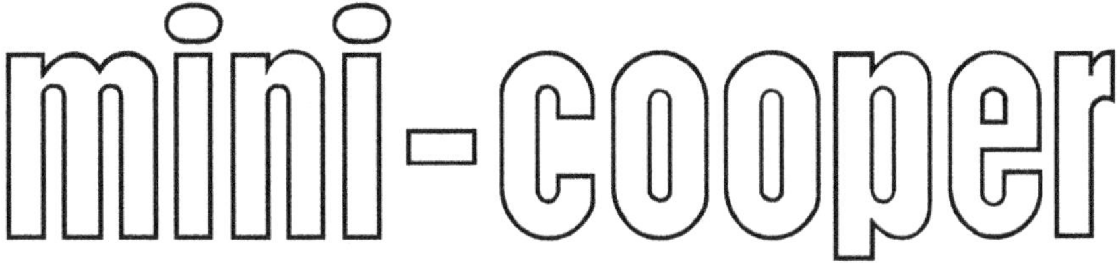

MINI-COOPER Mark II and MINI-COOPER S Mark II Handbook

The British Motor Corporation Limited

Longbridge, Birmingham, England

Publication Part No. AKD 4997

FOREWORD

This Handbook provides an introduction to your car together with information on the care and periodic maintenance required for trouble-free motoring with minimal running costs. The contents may include variations in the specification of some or all of the models shown on the front page. The Handbook does not in any way constitute a particular vehicle specification.

Your BMC Distributor or Dealer is provided with the latest information concerning special service tools and workshop techniques. This enables him to undertake your service and repairs in the most efficient and economic manner.

Owners are recommended to use the Maintenance Voucher Scheme. A Passport to Service containing service vouchers is provided and regular use of the vouchers in sequence is the best safeguard against the possibility of abnormal repair bills at a later date. Failure to have your car correctly maintained could invalidate the terms of the Warranty.

Completed voucher counterfoils are proof of regular servicing and could well enhance the value of your vehicle in the eyes of a prospective buyer. A replacement Passport to Service voucher book is obtainable from Distributors or Dealers.

Please note that references to right- or left-hand in this Handbook are made when viewing the car from the rear.

CONTENTS

CONTROLS

Fig. 1   **Left-hand drive**

Fig. 2   **Right-hand drive**

(1) (2) (3) **Pedals.** The pedals are arranged in the conventional positions.

The brake pedal operates the brake hydraulic system and applies the brakes on all four wheels, also bringing the stop warning lights into operation when the ignition is switched on.

(4) **Gear lever.** The gear positions are indicated on the lever knob. To engage reverse gear move the lever to the right in the neutral position until resistance is felt, apply further side pressure to overcome the resistance and then move it backwards to engage the gear. Synchromesh is provided on second, third, and fourth gears.

(5) **Hand brake.** The hand brake is of the pull-up lever type, operating mechanically on the rear wheels only. To release the hand brake pull the lever upwards slightly, depress the button on the end of the lever and push the lever down.

Fig. 1

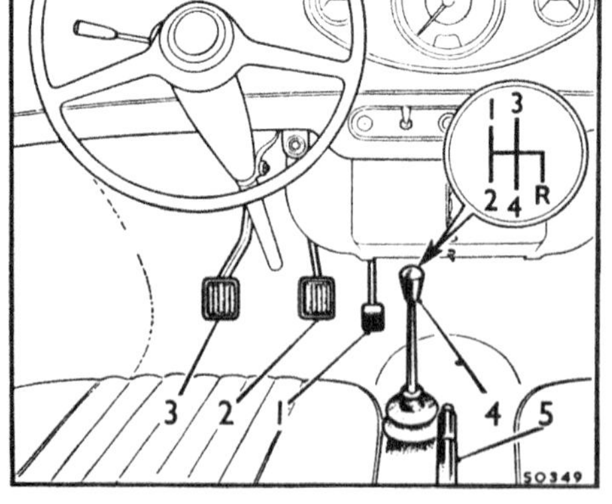

Fig. 2

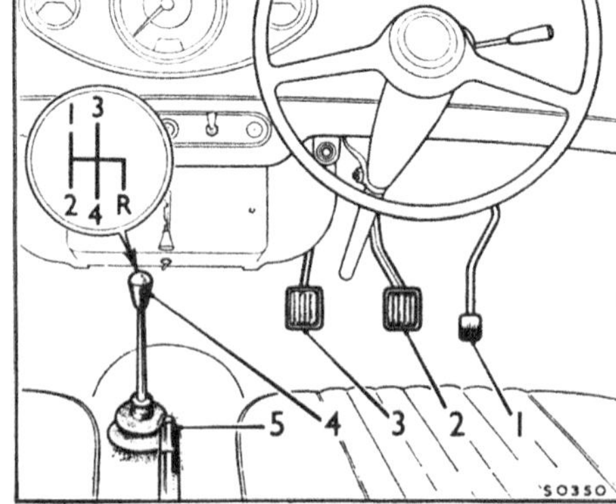

INSTRUMENTS AND SWITCHES

Fig. 1   Left-hand drive

Fig. 2   Right-hand drive

Direction indicator switch. The self-cancelling switch operates the indicators when the ignition is switched on. Move the lever to the (2) position to indicate left-hand turns and to (3) for right-hand turns.

Headlight flasher. The switch is integral with the direction indicator switch. Lifting the switch lever towards the steering-wheel (4) flashes the headlight main beams, when the headlights are switched off or are on in the dipped position.

Headlight beam dipping switch. The headlight beams are controlled by the combined direction indicator and headlight switch control lever when the headlights are switched on. Moving the lever to the (5) position provides high beam and returning the lever to (1) dips the headlight beams.

Horn switch. The horn is sounded by pressing the end of the direction indicator switch.

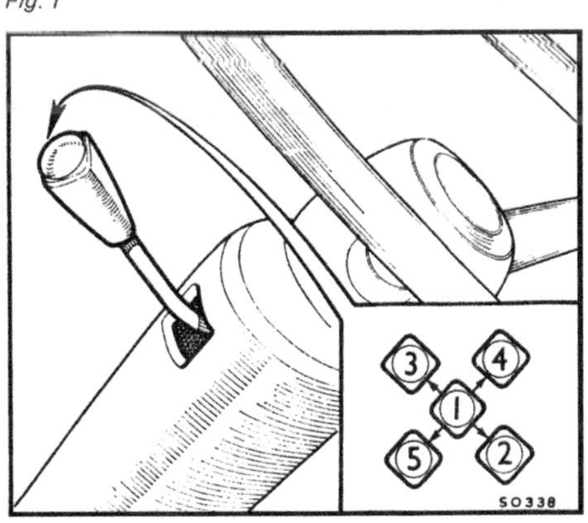

Fig. 1

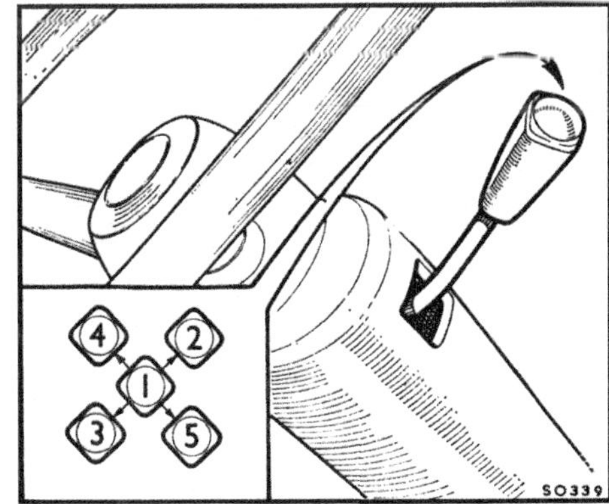

Fig. 2

Instruments and Switches

(1) **Direction indicator warning light (green).** The warning light will flash when the direction indicators are operating. In addition, the flasher unit will produce an audible 'tick' to remind the driver that the indicators are still flashing.

(2) (6) **Speedometer.** The instrument is graduated in m.p.h. and km.p.h. This will aid the driver to comply with speed regulations whilst driving in other countries. The speedometer also records the total distance the vehicle has travelled.

(3) **Coolant temperature gauge.** The gauge is marked 'C' indicating cold, 'N' indicating normal, and 'H' indicating hot. This is the temperature of the coolant leaving the cylinder head.

(4) **Oil filter warning light (amber).** The warning light is your guide to the need for a more frequent oil and filter change, see' **'RUNNING INSTRUCTIONS'**.

Fig. 3

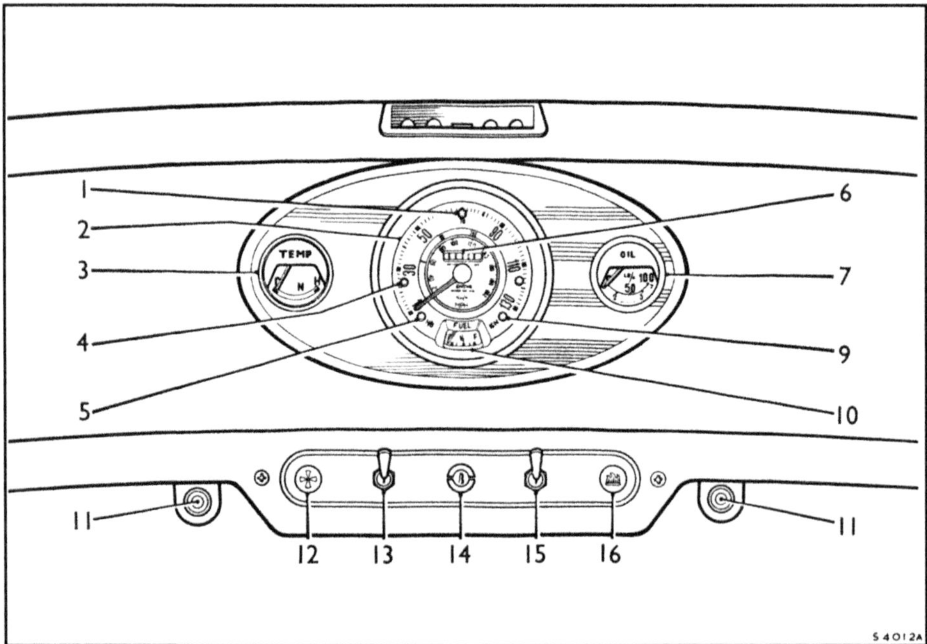

(5)   **Headlight main-beam warning light (blue).** The light glows when the headlights are switched on and the beam is in the raised position. The light goes out when the beam is dipped.

(7)   **Oil pressure gauge.** The gauge registers the pressure of the oil in the engine lubrication system. Important notes on its indications are given in '**RUNNING INSTRUCTIONS**'.

(9)   **Ignition warning light (red).** The light should glow with the ignition switched on, or at a slow idling speed. It should go out and stay out while the engine is running above normal idling speed.

(10)   **Fuel gauge.** When the ignition is switched on the fuel gauge indicates approximately the amount of fuel in the tank. An important note on filling with fuel is given in '**RUNNING INSTRUCTIONS**'.

(11)   **Windscreen washer.** Depress the washer control knob to obtain a spray of water/solvent mixture onto the windscreen. The washer control should be operated several times before switching on the windscreen wipers, particularly when following other vehicles under wet road conditions.

During cold weather the washer container should be filled with a recommended solvent/water mixture to prevent freezing. **On no account must radiator anti-freeze be used.**

(12)   **Mixture control (choke).** Pull out the control knob to assist starting when the engine is cold. The fuel/air mixture is progressively enriched as the control is pulled out.

Turn the knob to lock the control in position and release it by turning it in the reverse direction. Notes on use of the control are given in '**RUNNING INSTRUCTIONS**'.

(13)   **Windscreen wiper switch.** Move the switch lever down to bring both wiper blades into operation. The blades park automatically when the lever is raised to the off position.

(14)   **Ignition and starter switch.** The ignition and starter are both controlled by a single switch operated by a removable key. To switch on the ignition insert the key and turn it in a clockwise direction until a slight resistance is felt. Further movement in the same direction operates the starter motor. Release the key immediately the engine starts.

To reduce the possibility of theft ignition switches are *not* marked with a number. Owners are advised to make a note of the number stamped on their ignition key.

(15)   **Lighting switch.** Move the lever downwards to the first position to switch on the side, tail, and rear number-plate lights.

Move into the fully down position to operate the headlights.

(16)   **Heat control.** Full details of the control positions are given in 'HEATING AND VENTILATING'.

Fig. 4   **Interior lamp.** The interior lamp is situated centrally in the roof above the front seats. It is controlled by a switch on the lamp and also by an automatic switch fitted on each front door pillar. With both doors closed the light may be switched on or off with the switch on the lamp.

Fig. 5   **Heated back-light.** The heated back-light will only operate with the ignition 'on'.

The indicator light shows when the switch is in the 'on' position.

Fig. 4

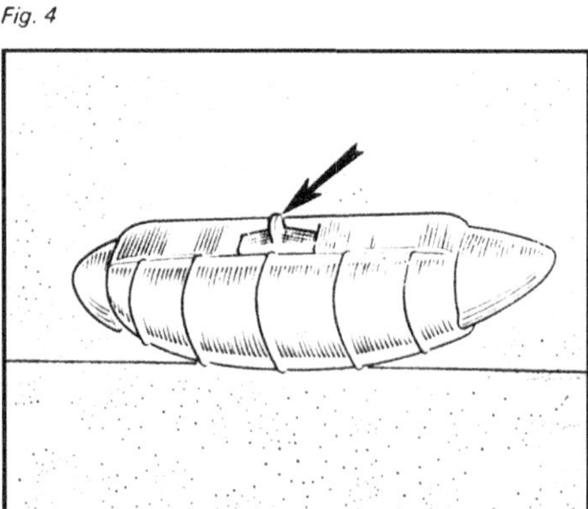

Fig. 5

RUNNING INSTRUCTIONS

Filling up with fuel When filling up with fuel avoid filling the tank until fuel is visible in the filler intake tube. Should this be done and the car left in the sun, there will be a considerable risk of fuel leakage due to expansion and consequent danger from exposed fuel. If inadvertently overfilled and the car is to be parked, take care to park it in the shade with the filler as high as possible.

Choice of fuel *H. C. engine* With the high-compression ratio engine it is essential that fuel with an octane rating (Research Method) of below 96 should not be used. Should it be necessary to use a lower-grade fuel, the car must be driven very carefully until the correct grade of fuel can be obtained.

It is recommended that fuel of 100-octane rating (Research Method) be used when optimum performance is required.

L.C. engine If the low-compression engine is fitted fuels of 91 to 96-octane rating (Research Method) should be used.

Starting Check that the gear lever is in the neutral position and the hand brake is applied. If the engine is cold pull out the mixture control (CHOKE). Switch on the ignition, check that the ignition warning light glows and operate the starter. As soon as the engine starts, release the ignition key and warm up the engine (see '**Warming up**'). Check that the oil pressure gauge is registering.

Warming up Warming up the engine by allowing it to idle slowly is harmful and leads to excessive cylinder wear. The correct procedure is to let the engine run fairly fast, approximately 1,000 r.p.m. corresponding to a speed of 15 m.p.h. (25 km.p.h.) in top gear, so that it attains its correct working temperature as quickly as possible. Far less damage is done by driving the car from cold than letting the engine idle slowly in the garage.

Running in The treatment given to a new car will have an important bearing on its subsequent life; engine and road speeds during this early period must be limited.

During the first 500 miles (800 km.) :
DO NOT exceed 45 m.p.h. (70 km.p.h.).
DO NOT operate at full throttle in any gear.
DO NOT allow the engine to labour in any gear.

After the running-in period, speeds should be progressively increased up to maximum performance.

Temperature gauge When the engine is running the gauge indicates the temperature of the coolant leaving the cylinder head.

When the ignition is switched off the needle returns to the 'cold' position.

As overheating may cause serious damage, the readings should be noted and after the initial rise in temperature during the warming up period any sudden upward change in the reading calls for immediate investigation.

Running Instructions

Ignition warning light
Fig. 1

The light (1) should glow when the ignition is switched on, and go out and stay out at all times while the engine is running above normal idling speed. Failure to do so indicates a fault in the battery charging system. Check that the fan belt is correctly tensioned before consulting your Distributor or Dealer.

Oil filter warning light
Fig. 1

If the light (2) comes on and continues to glow when the engine is running, the need for a new oil filter element and a change of engine oil is indicated; this should be carried out as soon as possible within a maximum of a further 300 miles (500 km.).

If 6,000 miles (10000 km.) or six months have passed since the last oil and filter element change, although the warning light has not come on, both engine oil and filter element must be changed.

Mixture control (choke)
Fig. 2

Push in the control completely immediately the engine will run evenly without its use. Always use the minimum setting for the shortest possible time. Do not use the choke when starting a warm engine.

The first $\frac{1}{4}$ in. (6 mm.) approximately of movement (A) opens the throttle slightly without affecting the mixture giving a fast engine idling speed.

Oil pressure gauge

The gauge should register immediately the engine is started and pressure may rise to approximately 70 lb./sq. in. (5 kg./cm.²). Under normal running conditions and temperatures the pressure should be 50 to 60 lb./sq. in. (3·5 to 4·2 kg./cm.²), with approximately 15 lb./sq. in. (1·05 kg./cm.²) at idling speed.

Should the gauge fail to register any pressure, stop the engine immediately and investigate the cause. Start by checking the oil level.

Fig. 1

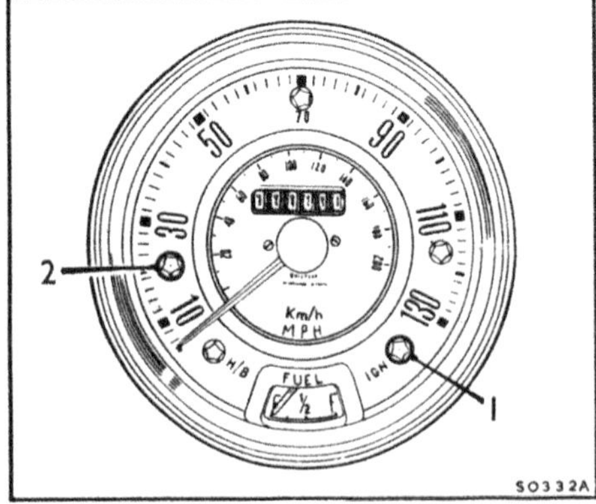

Fig. 2

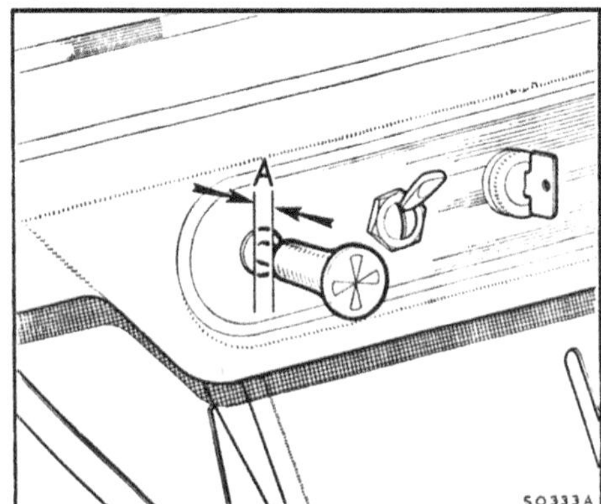

Wet brakes If the car has been washed or driven through water the brakes may be wet. To dry them, apply the brakes several times with the car moving slowly. Driving with wet brakes can be dangerous.

Keep the hand brake fully on when using high-pressure washing equipment.

Roof rack Bulky rather than heavy **loads no greater than 35 lb. (16 kg.) may be carried on a roof rack.** Remember that any load on the roof may affect the handling of the car, especially in a cross-wind or when cornering.

HEATING AND VENTILATING

Description The heating and ventilating system is designed to provide fresh air, either heated by the engine cooling system or at outside air temperature, to the car at floor level and, for demisting and defrosting, to the windscreen.

Air enters through a forward-facing intake; the ram effect caused by the car's motion provides air for the heater's requirements at speeds above 25 m.p.h. (40 km.p.h.). A blower motor controlled by the switch (3) is provided for use at lower speeds or when a greater quantity of air is required.

Heat control
Fig. 1 The heat control (1) on the switch panel controls the water valve and regulates the amount of hot water circulating the heating system. The maximum amount of heat is available when the knob is pushed fully in.

Intermediate positions of the control provide variations in temperature to meet changing conditions.
With the control pulled fully out, fresh air at outside air temperature will enter the interior when the car is in motion or if the blower unit is operated.

Air distribution
Fig. 1 Air distribution is controlled by the shutter lever (2) which can be set to the following positions.

Car: Air is directed mainly to the vehicle interior, with some to the windscreen.

Screen: Air is directed onto the windscreen, with some to the vehicle interior.

Off: The air supply is cut off.

Fresh-air unit This unit is similar to the fresh-air heater, except that the air supplied to the car is not heated. The air distribution control functions in the same way as that fitted to the fresh-air heater.

Frost precautions The heater unit cannot be drained with the cooling system, it is therefore essential to use anti-freeze in the cooling system in freezing conditions (see page 23).

Fig. 1

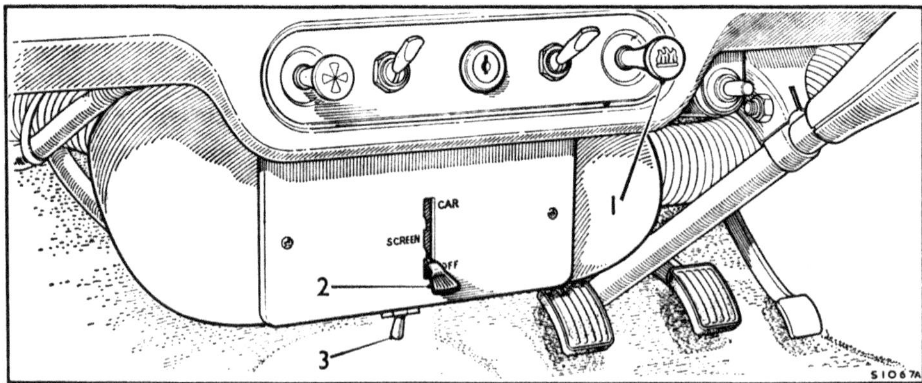

BODY AND FITTINGS

Door locks The driver's door is locked from the outside by using the ignition key.
Fig. 1

To unlock, turn the key towards the rear of the car and withdraw it.

To lock, turn the key towards the front of the car and withdraw it.

Fig. 2 The passenger's door may be locked from the inside by lifting up the small safety catch.

Front-sliding windows The door glasses may be partially opened by depressing the window catch (1) and sliding the glass to the desired position. A minimum opening of both the front sliding glasses will provide a draught-free ventilation and aid demisting in the winter.
Fig. 3

The door glasses may be locked in the closed position by ensuring that the window catch locking plungers (2) engage in the location holes (3) at each end of the window channel retaining strip.

Fig. 1

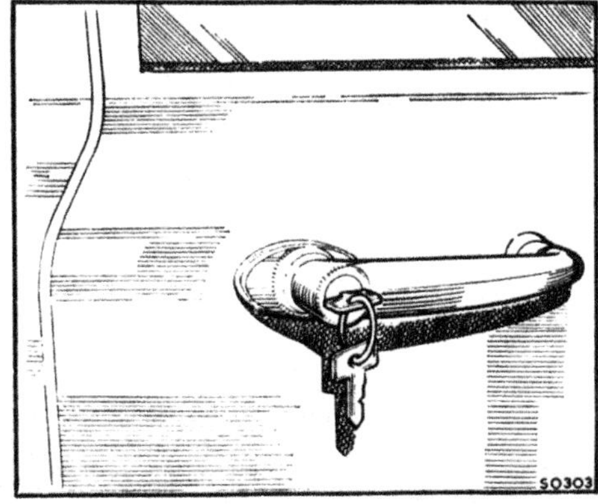

Fig. 2

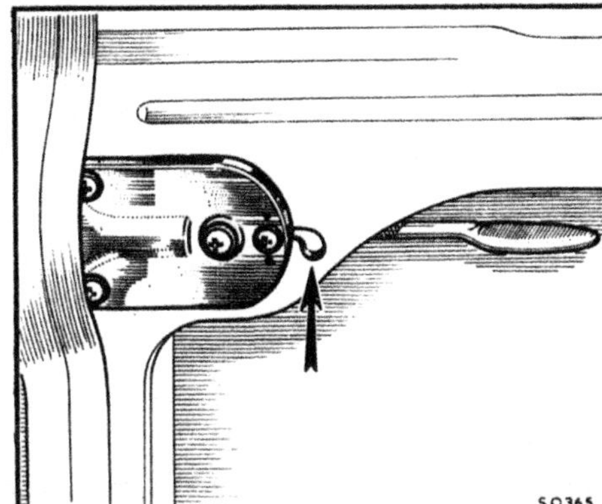

Fig. 3

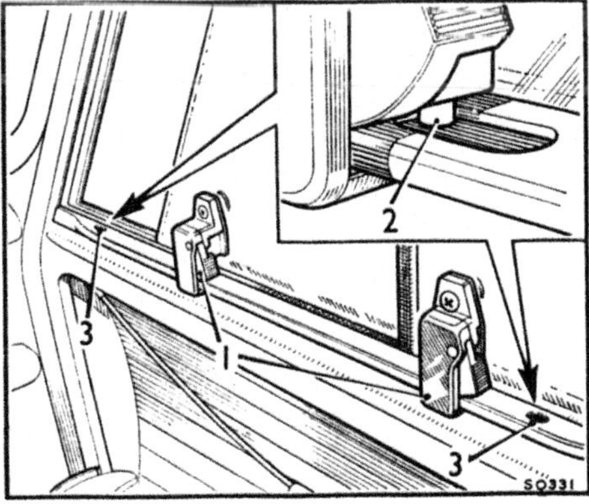

Fig. 4

Body and Fittings

Rear ventilators
Fig. 4

The rear ventilator windows are hinged at the front and are held in the closed position by a toggle catch.

To open a window, pull the catch forward and push outwards.

Close the window by pulling the centre of the catch inwards, and then pushing backwards until the catch is felt to snap into the locked position.

Bonnet
Figs. 5 and 6

Release the bonnet by moving the release lever (1) towards the right-hand side of the car, movement of the lever is assisted by applying downward hand pressure to the bonnet, push the safety catch (2) inwards and lift the bonnet. Release the bonnet stay (3) from its clip (4) and place the free end in the support bracket (5).

To close secure the stay in its clip and lower the bonnet. Apply double hand pressure to the front of the bonnet and press down. The safety catch and bonnet lock will be heard to engage.

Lubrication

Occasionally lubricate the door locks and hinges, safety catches, bonnet lock safety catch, and operating mechanism.

It is essential that the bonnet release mechanism and safety catch is adequately lubricated.

Fig. 5

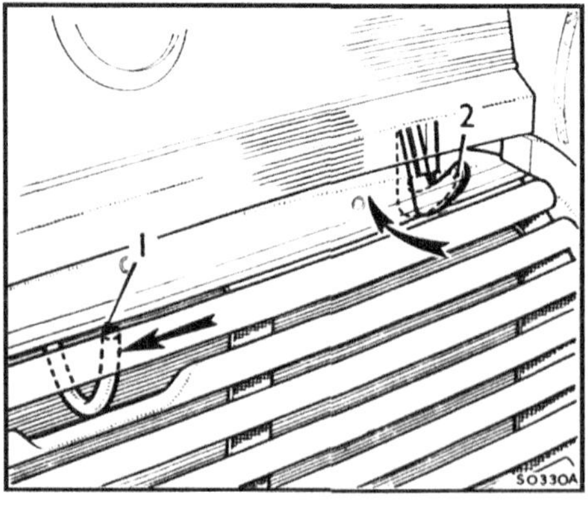

Fig. 6

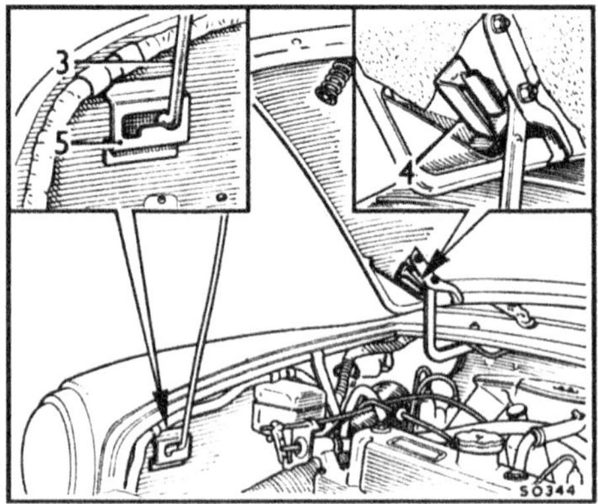

Luggage compartment Turn the handle in an anti-clockwise direction to release the catch. When closed turn the handle clockwise to secure.

The lid can be locked in the closed position with the ignition key.

Additional luggage-carrying capacity is provided by making use of the lid in the open position, and to allow this the rear number-plate is hinged.

Use the lid for carrying bulky rather than heavy articles.

Key numbers To reduce the possibility of theft the ignition switch and locks are not marked with a number. Owners are advised to make a note of the numbers on their keys in case of loss.

SEATS AND SEAT BELTS

SEATS

Adjustment
Fig. 1

Lift the spring-loaded lever (1) below the left-hand front corner of the seat and move the seat to the required position. Release the lever to lock the seat in position.

The range of seat adjustment can be extended by repositioning the seat on the front anchorage brackets (2) (rearmost position illustrated).

Adjustable squab
Fig. 2

The front seat squabs may be adjusted to variable rake positions.

Push the operating lever rearwards and move the seat squab to the required position. Release the lever to lock the squab in the selected position.

SEAT BELTS

Must be fitted by the Distributor or Dealer to attachment points incorporated in the car body. Two types of approved belts, i.e. Kangol Magnet 'static' and Britax 'automatic' are available for the front seats.

On all types, the short belt must be adjusted until the buckle is located to the side of the hip; see illustration).

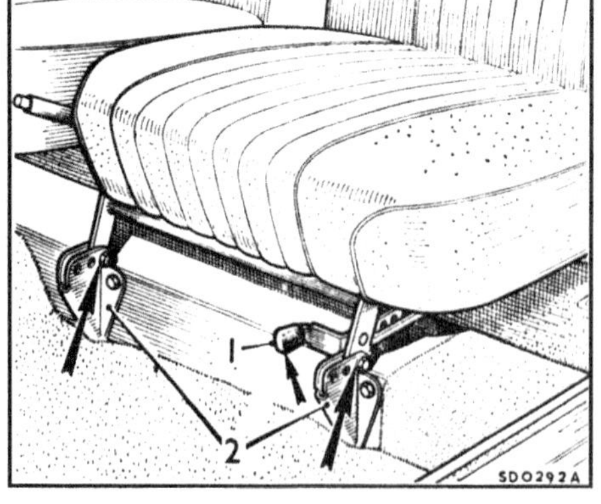

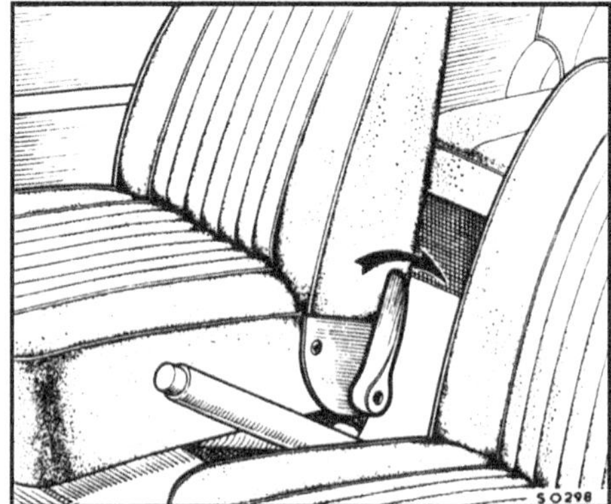

Static Ensure that the short belt used is attached to the side of the tunnel away from
Fig. 3 the wearer, i.e. the belt must cross the tunnel (1).

To fasten, lift the magnetic tongue (2) and engage the hook (3) with the
hinged part of the tongue.

To release, lift the buckle tongue outwards.

To adjust, use the belt adjuster on the door sill (4) and adjust until the lap
portion is comfortably tight and the diagonal belt passes over the chest, with
hand clearance between the belt and the chest.

To stow, attach the long belt hook onto the parking device (5) on the door
pillar attachment, stow the short belt by attaching the magnetic buckle to the
seat frame.

Automatic The automatic belt allows the wearer greater freedom of movement for normal
driving. During hard cornering or rapid deceleration, the reel locks the belt
immediately and restricts undue body movement of the wearer.

To fasten, push the tongue into the buckle until it is locked. This is indicated
by a positive 'click'.

To release, lift the front plate of the buckle while keeping a slight body pressure
against the belt.

To adjust, move the tongue on the long belt until the lap portion is comfortably
tight.

To stow, move the tongue on the long belt towards the door pillar pulley
bracket.

Fig. 3

CLEANING

Body Regular care of the body finish is necessary if the new appearance of the car exterior is to be maintained against the effects of air pollution, rain, and mud.

Wash the bodywork frequently, using a soft sponge and plenty of water containing a mild detergent. Large deposits of mud must be softened with water before using the sponge. Smears should be removed by a second wash in clean water, and with the sponge if necessary. When dry, clean the surface of the car with a damp chamois-leather. In addition to the regular maintenance, special attention is required if the car is driven in extreme conditions such as sea spray or on salted roads. In these conditions and with other forms of severe contamination an additional washing operation is necessary which should include underbody hosing. Any damaged areas should be immediately covered with paint and a complete repair effected as soon as possible. Before touching in light scratches and abrasions with paint thoroughly clean the surface. Use petrol/white spirit (gasoline/hydrocarbon solvent) to remove spots of grease or tar.
The application of BMC Car Polish is all that is required to remove traffic film and to ensure the retention of the new appearance.

Bright trim Never use an abrasive on stainless, chromium, aluminium, or plastic bright parts and on no account clean them with metal polish. Remove spots of grease or tar with petrol/white spirit (gasoline/hydrocarbon solvent) and wash frequently with water containing a mild detergent. When the dirt has been removed polish with a clean dry cloth or chamois-leather until bright. Any slight tarnish found on stainless or plated components which have not received regular attention may be removed with BMC Chrome Cleaner. An occasional application of mineral light oil or grease will help to preserve the finish, particularly during winter, when salt may be used on the roads, but these protectives must not be applied to plastic finishes.

Windscreen If windscreen smearing has occured it can be removed with BMC Screen Cleaner.

A razor blade will remove transfers from the window glass.

Interior Clean the carpets with a stiff brush or vacuum cleaner, preferably before washing the outside of the car. The most satisfactory way to give carpets a thorough cleaning is to apply BMC 2-way Cleaner with a semi-stiff brush, brush vigorously and remove the surplus with a damp cloth or sponge. Carpets should not be cleaned by the 'dry-clean' process. The upholstery and roof lining may be treated with BMC 2-way Cleaner applied with a damp cloth and a light rubbing action.

The BMC approved products mentioned above are obtainable from your Distributor or Dealer.

COOLING SYSTEM

Radiator filler cap The system is pressurized when hot, and the pressure must be released gradually when the filler cap is removed. It is advisable to protect the hands against escaping steam and turn the cap slowly anti-clockwise until the resistance of the safety stops is felt. Leave the cap in this position until all pressure is released. Press the cap downwards against the spring to clear the safety stops, and continue turning until it can be lifted off.

Draining Two drain plugs are provided in the cooling system. Carefully remove the radiator filler cap (if hot), and remove the drain plugs from the radiator (1) and from the rear of the cylinder block (2). Leave a reminder on the vehicle to the effect that the cooling system has been drained.

If the system contains anti-freeze, collect the coolant in a clean container for re-use.

Filling Refit the drain plugs and check hose connections.

To avoid wastage by overflow add just sufficient coolant to cover the bottom of the header tank. Run the engine until it is hot and add sufficient coolant to bring the surface to the level of the indicator positioned inside the header tank below the filler neck.

NOTE.—If a heater is fitted, push in the heat control to allow the water in the heating system to circulate when draining or filling the system.

Fig. 1

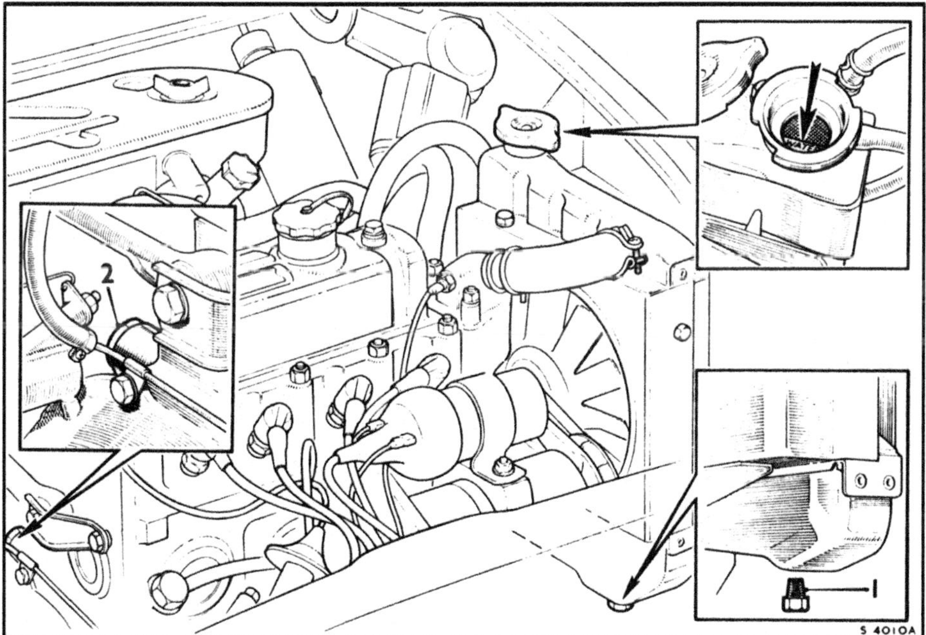

Cooling System

<table>
<tr><td>**Frost precautions**</td><td>Water, when it freezes, expands, and if precautions are not taken there is considerable risk of bursting the radiator, cylinder block, or heater (where fitted).</td></tr>
</table>

Only anti-freeze of the ethylene glycol type incorporating the correct type of corrosion inhibitor is suitable and owners are recommended to use Bluecol Anti-freeze. We also approve the use of any anti-freeze that conforms to Specification B.S.3151 or B.S.3152.

Before adding anti-freeze mixture the cooling system must be drained and flushed through by inserting a hose in the filling orifice and allowing water to flow through until clean. Refit the drain plugs and add the anti-freeze first.

Anti-freeze can remain in the cooling system for two years provided the specific gravity of the coolant is checked periodically and anti-freeze added as necessary. This operation should be carried out by an authorized Distributor or Dealer.

After the second winter the system should be drained and refilled with fresh water, and the appropriate amount of anti-freeze added when required.

The recommended quantities of anti-freeze solution are given below.

Do not use radiator anti-freeze solution in the windscreen-washing equipment. Use the correct washer solvent, which will not damage the paintwork.

Anti-freeze	*Commences to freeze*		*Frozen solid*		*Amount of anti-freeze*		
%	*°C.*	*°F.*	*°C.*	*°F.*	*Pts.*	*U.S. Pts.*	*Litres*
25	−13	9	−26	−15	1½	1·8	·85
33⅓	−19	−2	−36	−33	2	2·5	1·18
50	−36	−33	−48	−53	3¼	3·75	1·8

WHEELS AND TYRES

Jacking
Fig. 1
The jack is designed to lift one side of the car at a time. Apply the hand brake, and place a wedge against each side of one of the wheels on the opposite side of the car to the one being jacked.

Remove the plug from the jacking socket located in the door sill panel and insert the lifting arm of the jack into the socket. **Make certain that the jack lifting arm is pushed fully into the socket and that the base of the jack is on firm ground.** The jack should lean slightly outwards at the top to allow for the radial movement of the car as it is raised.

Jack maintenance
Neglect of the jack may lead to difficulty in a roadside emergency. Examine it occasionally, clean off accumulated dust, and lightly grease the thread to prevent rust.

Wheel trim removal
Remove the wheel trim from the road wheel with the flattened end of the wheel-brace inserted between the lip of the cover and the wheel rim. Lever the cover away from the wheel, using the tyre as a fulcrum at a point diametrically opposite the tyre valve.

Wheel removal
Apply the hand brake and block one or even two wheels remaining in contact with the ground.

Slacken the wheel nuts, raise the car with the jack to lift the wheel clear of the ground, remove the wheel nuts and withdraw the road wheel.

When refitting replace the nuts with the tapered ends towards the wheel and lightly tighten them with the wheel brace. Lower the jack and fully tighten the nuts progressively in diagonal sequence.

Fig. 1

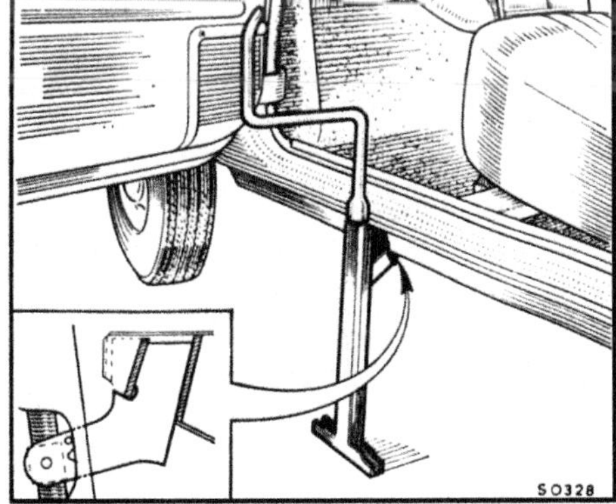

Fig. 2

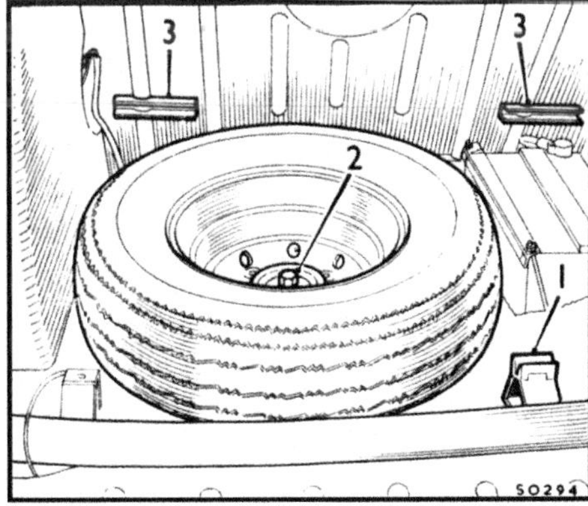

Wheels and Tyres

Spare wheel location
Fig. 2

The spare wheel is stowed in the well of the luggage compartment beneath the luggage platform floor.

Access to the spare wheel is obtained by lifting the rear edge of the floor board clear of the clamp (1), and withdrawing the floor from the luggage compartment.

The wheel can then be released by unscrewing the clamping bolt (2) with the wheel nut spanner.

When refitting, position the front edge of the floor into the two channel brackets (3) and press the retaining bracket on the rear edge into the rubber clamp.

Tyre pressures

Maintain the tyre pressures of all tyres including the spare to the figures given in 'GENERAL DATA'. Check with an accurate tyre gauge at least once a week.

Any unusual pressure loss should be investigated. Under-inflation causes rapid tyre wear, and even more serious is the possible damage to the cords of the fabric owing to excessive flexing of the cover walls.

Valves and caps

See that the valve caps are screwed down firmly by hand. Do not use tools as too much force will damage the rubber seating. The cap prevents the entry of dirt into the valve mechanism and forms an additional seal on the valve, preventing any leakage if the valve core is damaged.

Tyre care

Excessive local distortion as a result of striking a kerb, a loose brick, a deep pot-hole, etc., may cause the casing cords to fracture. Effort should be made to avoid such obstacles.

Flints and other sharp objects should be removed with a penknife or similar tool. If neglected, they may work through the tyre.

Penetration does not normally result in deflation if the object is not pulled out, and the tyres should be repaired when convenient. Penetration by objects of small diameter can be repaired with the tyre manufacturer's plugging kit.

The insertion of a plug to repair a puncture in a tubeless tyre must be regarded as a temporary measure and a permanent vulcanized repair must be made as soon as possible.

Any oil or grease which may get onto the tyres should be cleaned off by using petrol (fuel) sparingly. Do not use paraffin (kerosene), which has a detrimental effect on rubber.

Wheel and tyre balancing

Unbalanced wheel and tyre assemblies may be responsible for abnormal wear of the tyres and vibration in the steering. Consult your Distributor/Dealer.

<table>
<tr><td align="right">Changing
tyre positions
Fig. 3</td><td>To obtain the maximum mileage from tyres and to reduce irregular wear, interchange the front and rear wheels and bring the spare into use at intervals as advised by your Distributor/Dealer.</td></tr>
<tr><td align="right">Radial-ply
tyres (SP)</td><td>Cooper. Tubeless SP41 radial-ply tyres are fitted as standard equipment and all replacements must be of radial-ply construction.

Cooper 'S'. Tubed SP41 radial-ply tyres are fitted and replacements must also be tubed and of radial-ply construction.</td></tr>
<tr><td align="right">Tyre
replacement
Fig. 4</td><td>Tyre removal and refitting can only be carried out over the inner rim of the road wheel: tyres cannot be removed or refitted over the outer rim.

A white or coloured spot in the neighbourhood of the bead will indicate the lightest point of the tyre. This spot should be fitted in line with the valve to ensure the best wheel balance.

Initial inflation can be carried out with a foot pump and a rope tourniquet around the periphery of the tyre to obtain a seal between the tyre edge and the wheel rim, but it is more easily accomplished with a compressed air line.</td></tr>
</table>

Fig. 3

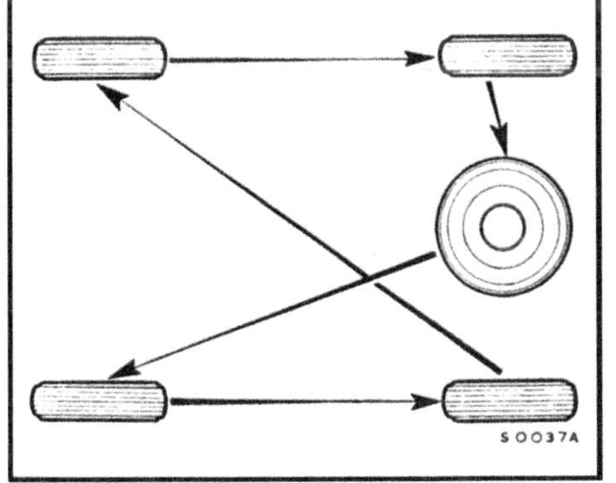

Fig. 4

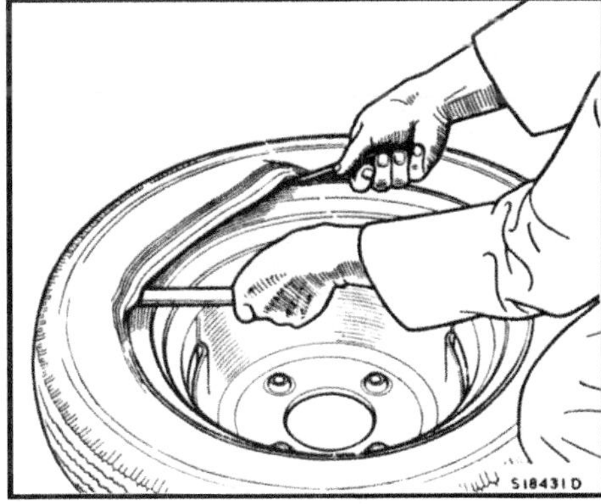

Master cylinder   Checking the fluid level is given with the clutch master cylinder on page 39.

Front brakes   Wear of the disc brake friction pads is automatically compensated for and manual adjustment is therefore not required. When the lining material has worn down to the minimum permissible thickness of $\frac{1}{16}$ in. (1·6 mm.) the brake pads must be renewed.

Special equipment is required, and new pads should be fitted by an authorized Distributor or Dealer.

Rear brakes   Excessive brake pedal travel is an indication that the rear brake-shoes require adjusting. The brakes on both rear wheels must be adjusted to regain even and efficient braking.

Adjusting   Block the front wheels, fully release the hand brake and jack up each rear
Fig. 1   wheel in turn. Turn the adjuster (arrowed) in a clockwise direction (viewed from the centre of the car) until the wheel is locked, then turn the adjuster back until the wheel is free to rotate without the shoes rubbing. Repeat the adjustment on the other rear brake.

Hand brake   The hand brake is automatically adjusted with the rear brakes. If there is excessive movement of the hand brake lever, consult your Distributor or Dealer.

Servo filter   **Cooper 'S'.** Clean the servo filter every 12,000 miles (20000 km.) or 12 months.
Fig. 2

Detach the air valve cover by removing the screws (arrowed) and push the air valve off its seat, (located in the underside of the cover). Blow compressed air at low pressure into the filter chamber. Do not lubricate or attempt to remove the filter from the air valve cover.

Fig. 1

Fig. 2

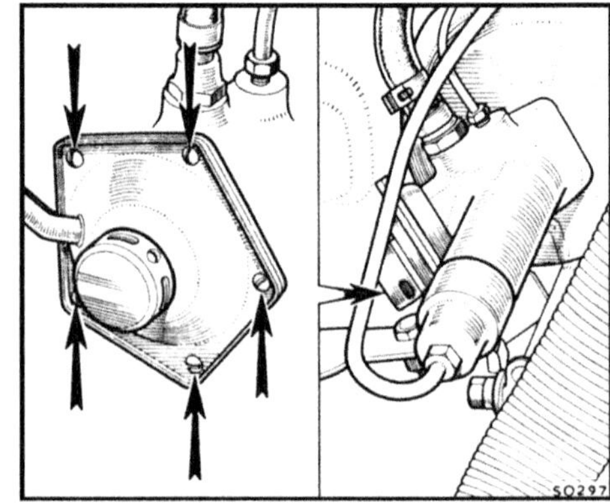

<table>
<tr><td>Inspect rear
brake linings</td><td>Block the front wheels, release the hand brake, and jack up each rear wheel in turn. Remove the road wheel, slacken off the brake-shoe adjuster fully, remove the two cross-head screws, and withdraw the brake-drum.</td></tr>
</table>

Inspect the linings for wear, and blow out any dust from the backplate assembly and drum.

Replace the drum and road wheel and adjust the brake-shoes.

<table>
<tr><td>Brake relining</td><td>When it becomes necessary to renew the brake linings it is essential that the material used is the same as that originally specified, or an approved alternative. under no circumstances must linings of varying materials be used at different brake stations. Replacement brake-shoes are obtainable from your Distributor under the Factory Exchange Unit Scheme, see page 53.</td></tr>
</table>

<table>
<tr><td>Preventive
maintenance</td><td>In addition to the recommended periodical inspection of brake components it is advisable as the car ages, and as a precaution against the effects of wear and deterioration, to make a more searching inspection and renew parts as necessary.</td></tr>
</table>

It is recommended that:
(1) Disc brake pads, drum brake linings, hoses, and pipes should be examined at intervals no greater than those laid down in the Passport to Service.
(2) Brake fluid should be changed completely every 18 months or 24,000 miles (40000 km.) whichever is the sooner.
(3) All fluid seals in the hydraulic system and all flexible hoses should be examined and renewed if necessary every 3 years or 40,000 miles (65000 km.) whichever is the sooner. At the same time the working surface of the pistons and of the bores of the master cylinder, wheel cylinders, and other slave cylinders should be examined and new parts fitted where necessary.

Care must be taken always to observe the following points:
(a) At all times use the recommended brake fluid.
(b) Never leave fluid in unsealed containers. It absorbs moisture quickly and this can be dangerous.
(c) Fluid drained from the system or used for bleeding is best discarded
(d) The necessity for absolute cleanliness throughout cannot be over-emphasized.

Battery location — The battery is located in the well of the luggage compartment.

Access to the battery is obtained by lifting the rear edge of the floor board clear of the clamp and withdrawing the floor from the luggage compartment.

When refitting, position the front edge of the floor into the two channel brackets and press the retaining bracket on the rear edge into the rubber clamp.

Topping up — Wipe away all dirt and moisture from the top of the battery. Check that the
Fig. 1 terminals are secure and smear with petroleum jelly.

Remove the manifold (1) and examine the level of the electrolyte in each cell. If necessary, add distilled water until the perforated separator guard (2) is just covered. **Do not overfill.** More frequent 'topping up' may be necessary in hot climates or if long daily runs are made.

Do not use tap-water and do not use a naked light when examining the condition of the cells.

Never leave the battery in a discharged condition for any length of time. When not in regular use have the battery fully charged, and every fortnight give it a short refreshing charge to prevent any tendency for the plates to become permanently damaged.

Specific gravity — The specific gravity of the electrolyte in each cell must be checked. This should be done by your Distributor/Dealer who can make adjustments if required.

Fig. 2 **Cooper**

Fig. 3 **Cooper 'S'**

Fuses — The fuse holder is situated on the right-hand side of the engine bulkhead and is covered by a plastic push-on cover (1).

Fig. 1

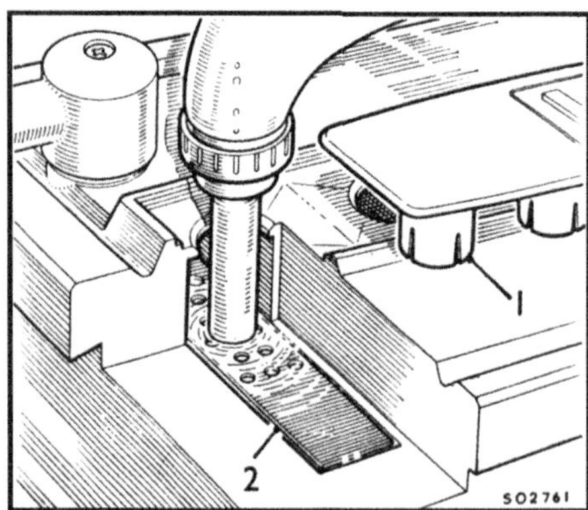

Fig. 2

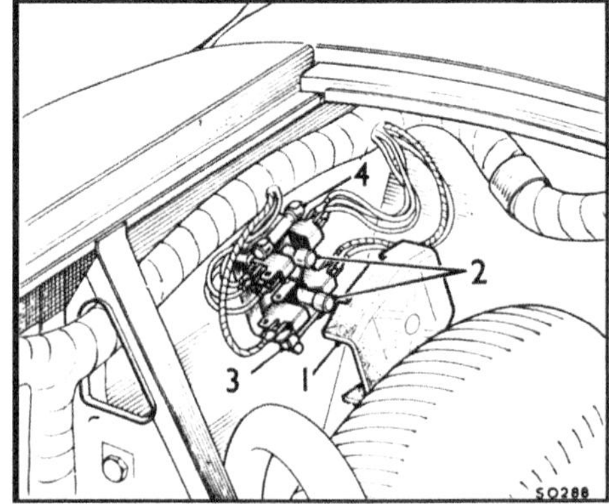

| **Spare fuses** | Two spare fuses (2) are provided in the fuse holder. It is important to use only the correct replacement fuse, and the fusing value is marked on a paper slip inside the glass tube of the fuse. |

Fuse connecting 'A1' and 'A2' The auxiliary units protected by this 35-amp. fuse (3) are the interior light and the horn, which will operate without the ignition switched on.

The fitting of additional accessories which are required to operate independently of the ignition circuit should be connected into the 'A2' terminal. Fitted car radios are protected further by their own line fuse.

Fuse connecting 'A3' and 'A4' This 35-amp. fuse (4) protects the auxiliary units which operate only when the ignition is switched on. The units connected into this circuit are the flashing direction indicators, windscreen wiper motor, heater blower motor and the brake/stop lights.

If additional accessories are fitted which are to be operated only when the ignition is switched on, these should be connected into the 'A4' terminal. This will also ensure that the accessory is not left switched on when the vehicle is garaged or parked.

Side/tail lamp fuse
Fig. 4 This 35-amp. line fuse protects the side and tail lighting circuit. It is located in a cylindrical tube adjacent to the wiring connectors on the engine bulkhead.

To renew the fuse, hold one end of the tube, push in, twist and pull off the other end. The fuse is then accessible for replacement.

Fuse replacement A blown fuse is indicated by the failure of all the units protected by it, and is confirmed by examination when withdrawn.

Before renewing a blown fuse inspect the wiring of the units that have failed for evidence of a short circuit or other fault. If the new fuse blows immediately and the cause of the trouble cannot be found, have the circuit checked by a Distributor or Dealer.

Fig. 3

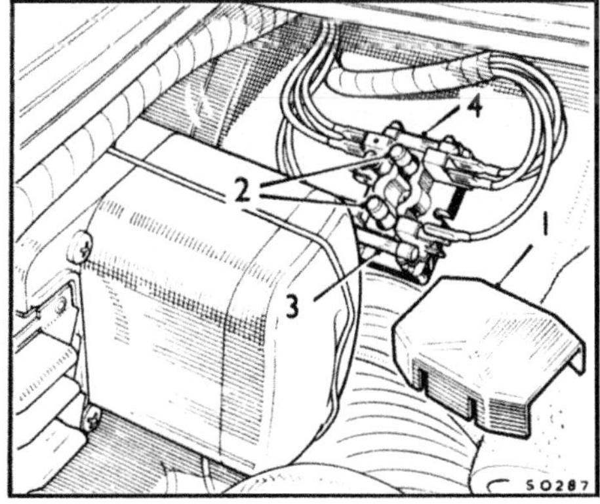

Fig. 4

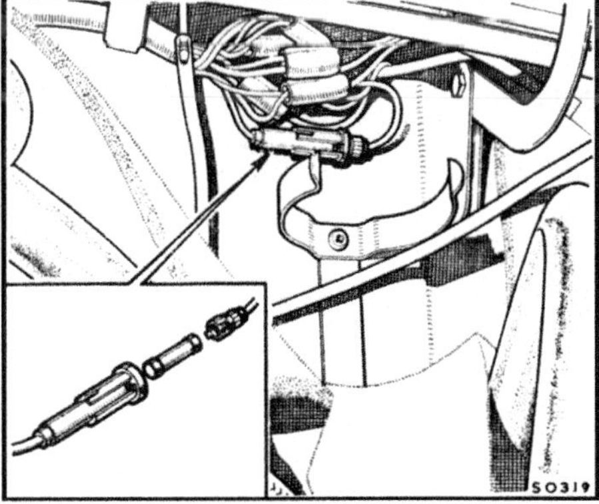

Electrical

<table>
<tr><td>Headlamp
light unit</td><td>Sealed-beam or renewable-bulb light units are used, with alternative types of bulb holders, the type fitted being dependent on the lighting regulations existing in the country for which the car was produced.</td></tr>
<tr><td>Replacement</td><td>The method of gaining access to the light unit for replacement is the same for both types. The different types of bulbs and holders are shown in Fig. 5.</td></tr>
</table>

Removing : Ease the bottom of the outer rim (1) forward away from the lamp, and lift it off the retaining lugs at the top of the lamp. Unscrew the three inner rim retaining screws (2) remove the inner rim (3) and withdraw the light unit (4).

Sealed-beams. Withdraw the three-pin connector (5) or (6) from the back of the reflector, and remove the light unit.

Headlamp pilot lamp (6). Withdraw the holder from the light unit and pull out the capless bulb.

Spring clip type (7). Withdraw the three-pin connector, disengage the spring clip from the reflector lugs, and withdraw the bulb. Fit the new bulb into the reflector, ensuring that the pip on the bulb flange, engages the slot in the reflector. Refit the spring clip ensuring that the coils in the clip are resting on the base of the bulb and that the legs of the clip are fully engaged under the reflector lugs. Refit the three-pin connector.

Fig. 5

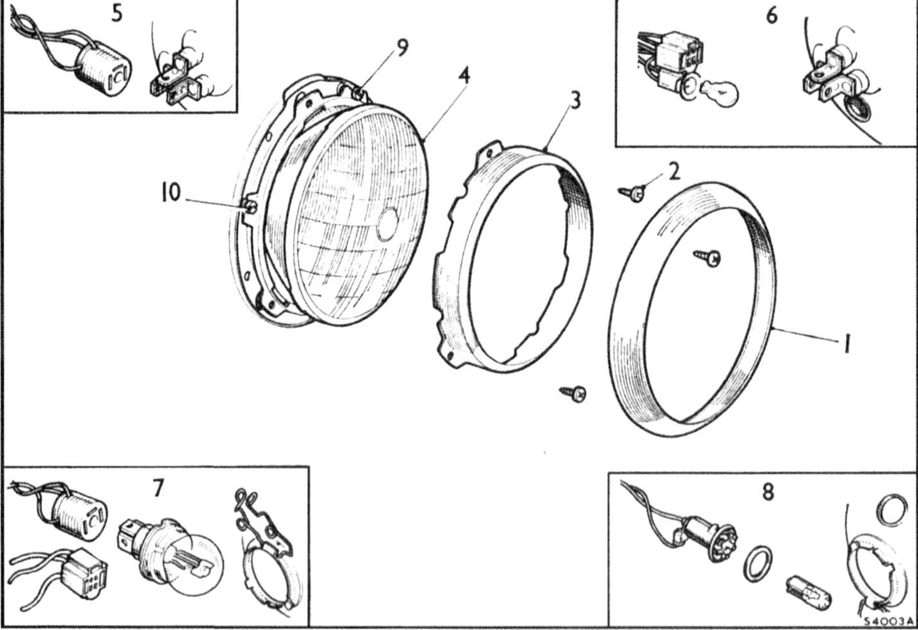

Headlamp pilot lamp (8). Withdraw the holder from the reflector, press and turn the bulb anti-clockwise and withdraw it from the holder. Engage the pins of the new bulb in the grooves of the holder, press and turn the bulb clockwise. Press the holder into its hole in the reflector.

Refitting. Locate the three lugs on the rear outer edge of the light unit in the slots formed in the lamp body, and refit the inner rim and its retaining screws. Position the outer rim on the retaining lugs at the top of the lamp, and press the rim downwards and inwards.

Beam setting

Two adjusting screws are provided on each headlamp for setting the main beams. The screw (9) is for adjusting the beam in the vertical plane, and the screw (10) is for horizontal adjustment. The beams must be set in accordance with local regulations; resetting and checking should be entrusted to your Distributor or Dealer, who will have special equipment available for this purpose.

Side and direction indicator lamps
Fig. 6

Vehicles built for certain countries have combined side and direction indicator lights. These are fitted with a double filament bulb which have offset locating pegs to avoid incorrect bulb replacement.

To replace the bulb, turn back the rubber sealing flanges and remove the plated rim and the glass, the bulb may then be withdrawn. When refitting ensure that the rim and the glass are correctly secured by the rubber flange.

Front direction indicator lamps

Bulb replacement is the same as described for 'side and direction indicator lamps', except that the bulbs have a single filament and therefore the locating pegs are not offset.

Number-plate lamp
Fig. 7

Access to the bulbs (1) is obtained by unscrewing the one slotted screw and removing the domed cover (3) and glass (2).

Fig. 6

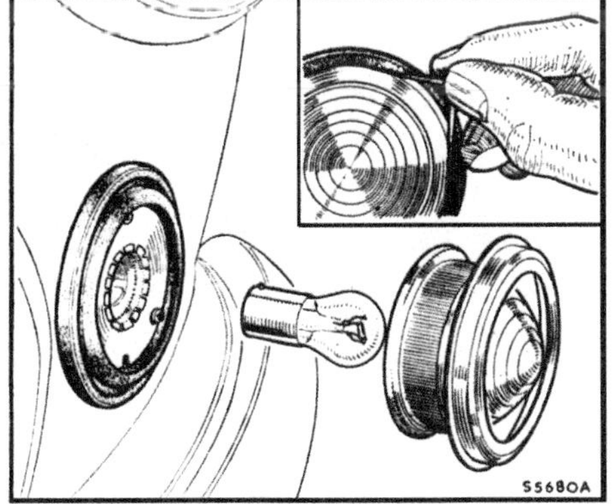

Fig. 7

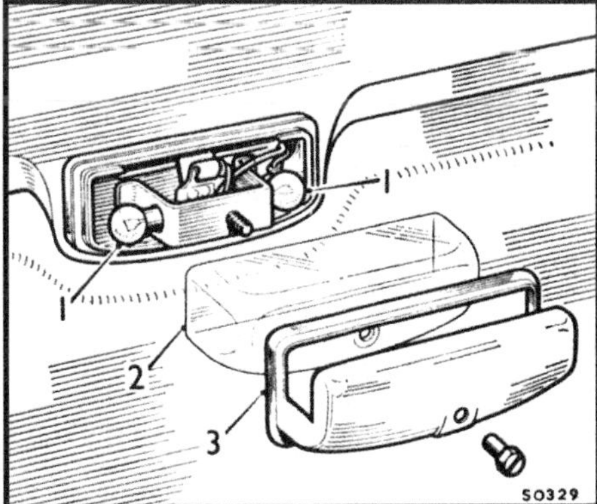

Electrical

Stop/tail and direction indicator lamps
Fig. 8

To renew a bulb, remove the three screws (3) and withdraw the lamp lenses.

The direction indicator bulb (1) is fitted in the top and the stop/tail lamp bulb (2) in the lower compartment. The latter is of the double-filament type giving a marked increase in illumination on brake application to provide a stop warning.

This bulb has offset locating pins to ensure correct replacement.

Interior lamp
Fig. 9

To renew a bulb, squeeze the two sides of the plastic lens together until the retaining lugs of the lens (1) are clear of the sockets in the lamp base. The lens can then be withdrawn and the festoon-type bulb (2) pulled out of its holder.

Dynamo lubrication
Fig. 10

To lubricate the dynamo add a few drops of oil through the central hole in the rear bearing housing. Avoid overlubrication.

Fig. 8

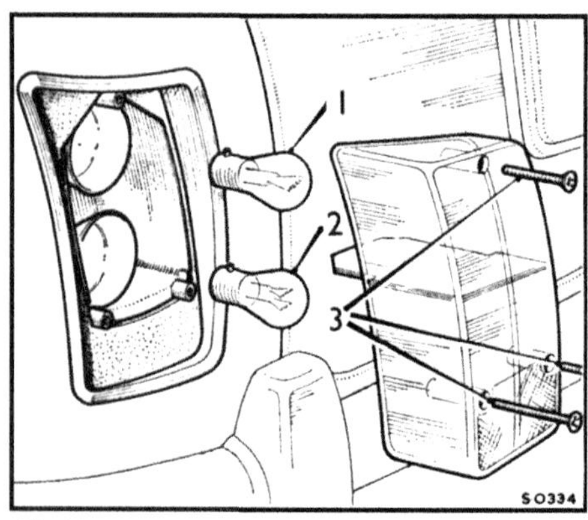

Fig. 9

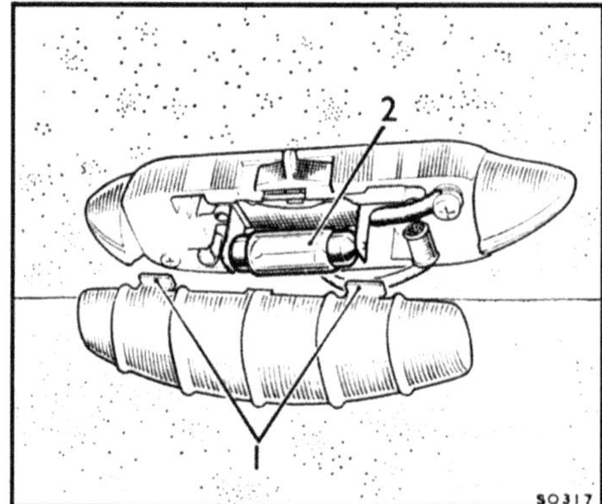

Fig. 10

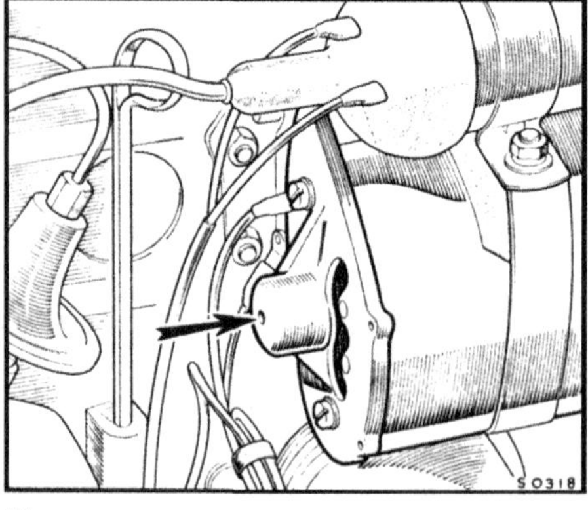

Fig. 11

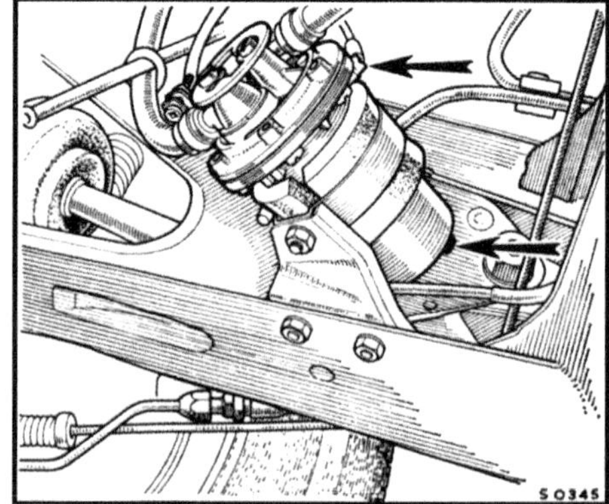

Fuel pump Fuel is delivered to the carburetter by an S.U. electric fuel pump. The pump is
Fig. 11 mounted on the left-hand side-member of the rear under-frame, and is
accessible from beneath the car.

Should the pump fail, check the electrical feed and earth connections (arrowed)
on the pump body to ensure they are making good contact and that the
retaining nuts are reasonably tight.

Panel and Access to the speedometer illuminating light and the warning light bulbs is
warning lights effected from under the bonnet. Remove the carburetter air cleaner (see page
Fig. 12 38) and pull the felt sound blanket away from the speedometer aperture.
Withdraw the push-in-type holders from the rear of the speedometer and the
temperature and oil pressure gauges for bulb replacement.

Refit the felt sound blanket and the carburetter air cleaner.

		Volts	Watts	BMC Part No.
Replacement bulbs	Headlamps, R.H.D. (dip left)	12	50/40	BFS 414
	Headlamps, L.H.D. (except Europe—dip right)	12	50/40	BFS 415
	Headlamps, Europe (except France—dip vertical)	12	45/40	BFS 410
	Headlamps, France (dip vertical)	12	45/40	BFS 411
	Pilot lamps	12	6	BFS 989
	Pilot lamps (capless-type bulbs)	12	5	BFS 501
	Pilot lamps and front flashing direction indicators	12	21/6	BFS 380
	Flashing direction indicators—front (U.K. only)	12	21	BFS 382
	Flashing direction indicators—rear	12	21	BFS 382
	Number-plate lamp	12	6	BFS 989
	Panel and warning lights	12	2·2	BFS 987
	Direction indicator warning light	12	2·2	BFS 987
	Tail and stop lamps	12	21/6	BFS 380
	Interior lamp (when fitted)	12	6	BFS 254

Fig. 12

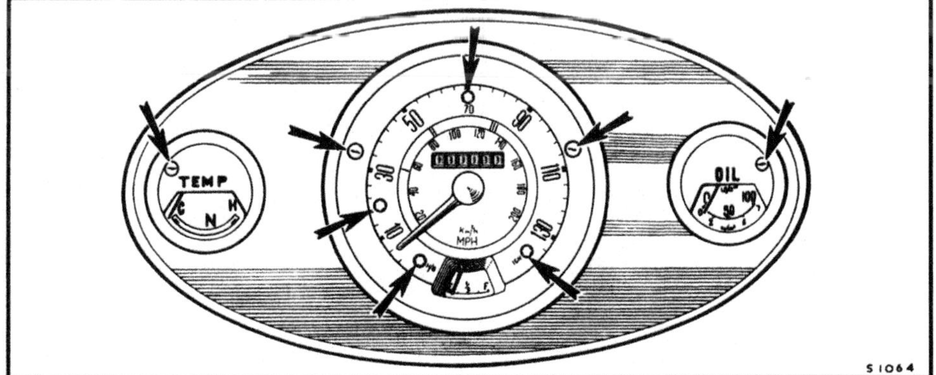

Electrical

Voltage regulator This is a sealed unit, located on the right-hand wing valance, which controls the charging rate of the dynamo in accordance with the needs of the battery. It requires no attention and should not be disturbed.

Starter
Fig. 13 The starter motor is mounted on the right-hand side of the engine on the flywheel housing. It requires no lubrication between overhaul periods.

Should the starter pinion become jammed with the flywheel ring, it can usually be freed by turning the squared end of the armature spindle with a spanner.

Windscreen wiper Motor This unit does not normally require adjustment, it is prepacked with grease and does not require further lubrication.

Arms
Fig. 14 To reposition a wiper arm on the spindle, the arm can be withdrawn when the small spring clip (1) is held clear of the retaining groove. Replace the arm in the required position and push it hard down onto the spindle (2) until it is secured in position by the retaining clip.

Blade replacement To renew a wiper blade pull the wiper arm away from the windscreen and withdraw the blade from the arm with a gentle outward curving pull. Insert the end of the curved 'wrist' of the arm into the slotted spring fastener of the new blade, and swivel the blade into engagement with the arm.

To remove the blade rubber depress the retaining pin on the outer end of the blade and slide the rubber out of the retainer clips.

Blade rubbers should be renewed each year.

Fig. 13

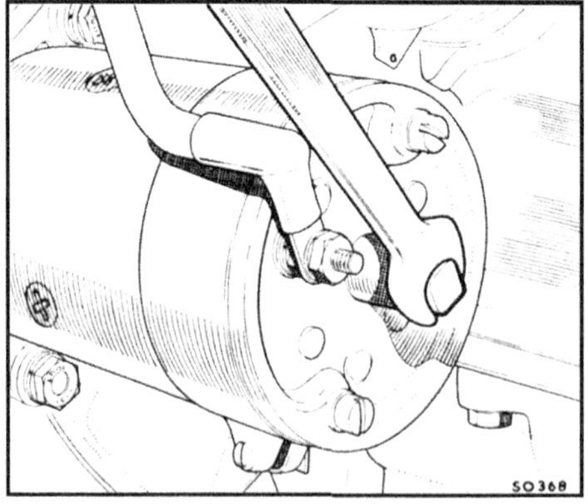

Fig. 14

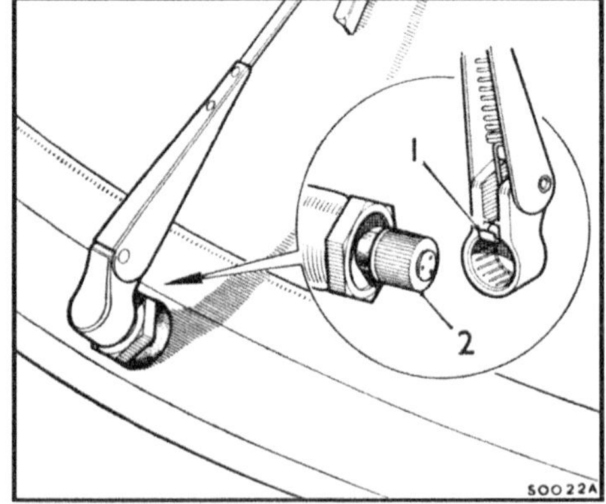

Distributor Check the functioning of the automatic advance and retard mechanism as follows.

Advance mechanism
Fig. 1

Centrifugal: Remove the distributor cover and grasp the rotor arm (1) firmly. Turn the rotor in the direction of rotation and release it. The rotor arm should return to its original position without showing any tendency to stick.

Vacuum: Using a screwdriver, check that the plate (2) moves easily and smoothly to ensure that the vacuum-operated advance mechanism can operate.

Contact breaker
Fig. 2

Remove the distributor cap and turn the crankshaft until the contacts are fully open. Check the gap (1) with a feeler gauge (see '**GENERAL DATA**'); the gauge should be a sliding fit in the gap. If the gap varies appreciably from the gauge thickness, slacken the contact plate securing screw (2) and adjust the contact gap by inserting a screwdriver in the notched hole at the end of the plate (3) and turning clockwise to decrease and anti-clockwise to increase the gap. Retighten the securing screw.

If the contact breaker points are burned or blackened, clean them with a fine carborundum stone or with fine emery-cloth.

Cleaning the contacts is made easier if the contact breaker lever carrying the moving contact is removed. To do this unscrew the nut securing the end of the spring, remove the spring washer, flat washer, and both lead terminals, and lift off the lever complete with spring. After cleaning refit the contact breaker and check the gap.

Thoroughly wipe the distributor cap to ensure that it is clean and check the carbon brush for free movement.

Fig. 1

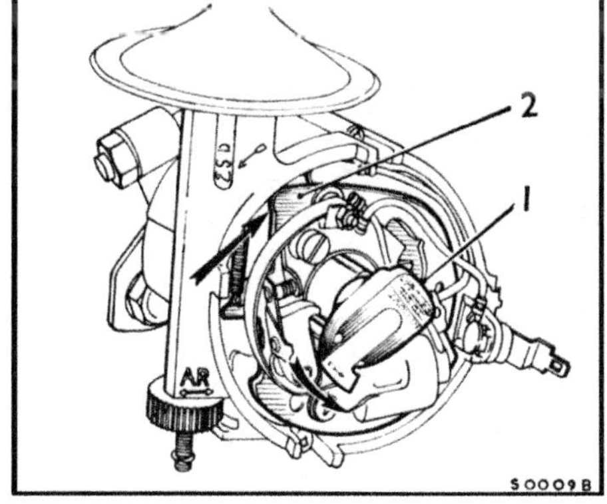

Fig. 2

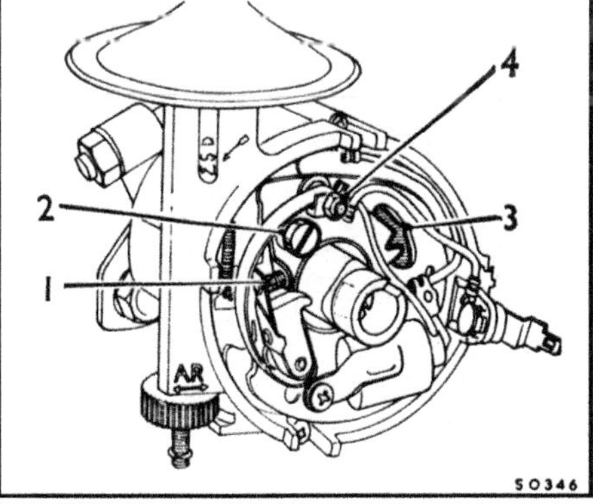

Ignition

Lubrication
Fig. 3
Remove the distributor cover and rotor arm and lightly smear the cam (1) with grease or oil. Avoid over-lubricating.

Place a drop of oil or grease on the contact breaker pivot (2).

Add a few drops of oil to the following points: Through the hole (3) in the contact breaker plate to lubricate the centrifugal weights. Around the screw (4) in the centre of the cam spindle (do not remove this screw as clearance is provided for oil to pass).

Carefully wipe away all surplus oil and see that the contact breaker points are perfectly clean and free of oil. Refit the rotor with its drive spindle engaging the spindle slot and push it on the shaft as far as it will go. Wipe the cover clean, and replace.

Sparking plugs
Fig. 4
The sparking plugs should be cleaned, preferably with an air-blast service unit, and the gaps reset to ·025 in. (·64 mm.).

Use a special Champion sparking plug gauge and setting tool and move the side electrode on the plug, never the centre one.

When fitting new sparking plugs ensure that only the recommended type (see 'GENERAL DATA') is used and that they are set to the correct gap before installation.

Static ignition timing
The point where ignition should start is given in 'GENERAL DATA'. With the crankshaft stationary at this position the contact breaker points should be just beginning to open. When the engine is running timing is varied by a centrifugal advance mechanism.

Check that the contact points are set to the correct gap when on the peak of the distributor cam (see 'GENERAL DATA').

The information given on page 35 describes a method of checking the ignition timing; it does not detail the resetting of the timing when the distributor has been removed from the engine.

Fig. 3

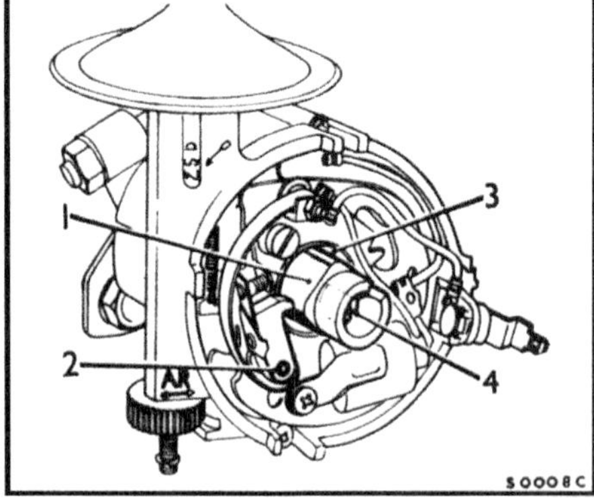

Fig. 4

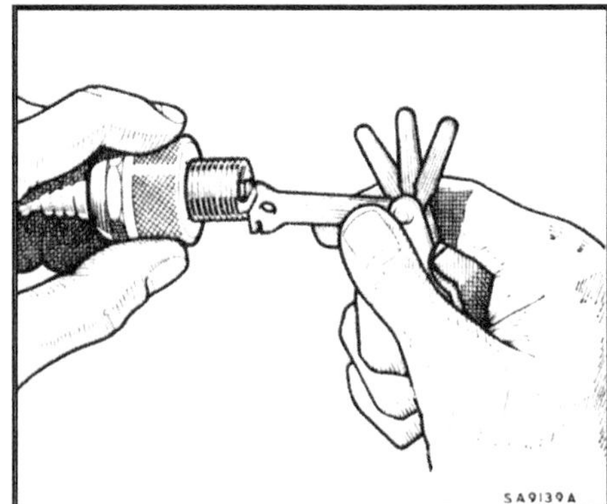

Checking *Fig. 5*	Remove the inspection cover from the top of the clutch housing and, with a mirror, look for the small pointer projecting below the top of the opening.

Four marks are provided on the flywheel face: 1/4, which is the T.D.C. position for Nos. 1 and 4 cylinders, and three further marks giving 5°, 10°, and 15° B.T.D.C.

To turn the flywheel to the required position remove the sparking plugs, engage top gear and push the car forward. Align the small pointer on the clutch housing with the correct mark on the flywheel (see 'GENERAL DATA').

With the crankshaft in this position the contact points should be just about to open.

Adjusting
Fig. 6

Cooper. If the points are open, turn the knurled nut (arrowed) towards 'R' until they are closed, then turn the nut in the reverse direction until the points just part. If the points are closed, turn the nut towards 'A' until they just part.

A simple electrical method may be used to ensure an accurate check. Connect a 12-volt bulb between the low-tension terminal on the side of the distributor and a good earth point on the engine. Switch on the ignition. If the bulb lights, turn the knurled nut towards 'R' until the light goes out and then back towards 'A' until it just lights. If the bulb does not light, turn the nut towards 'A' until it just lights. This will give the correct static timing.

Cooper 'S'. There is no vacuum advance unit on the distributor and therefore no adjuster knob for final adjustment of the ignition point.

If the points are open, slacken the distributor clamp screw (1) and turn the distributor body in the direction of the arrow 'R' (anti-clockwise) until they are closed; if they are closed, turn the distributor in the direction of the arrow 'A' (clockwise). In both cases turn the distributor until the points are just parting. Tighten the distributor clamp screw.

The electrical method of checking described above for the **'Cooper'** is also applicable, except that adjustment is effected by turning the distributor body.

Fig. 5

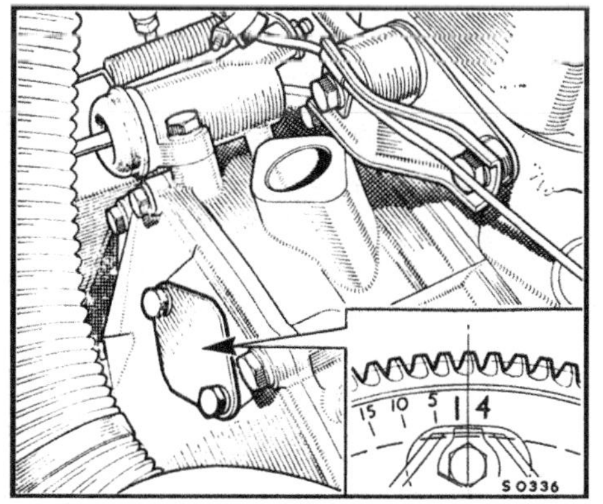

Fig. 6

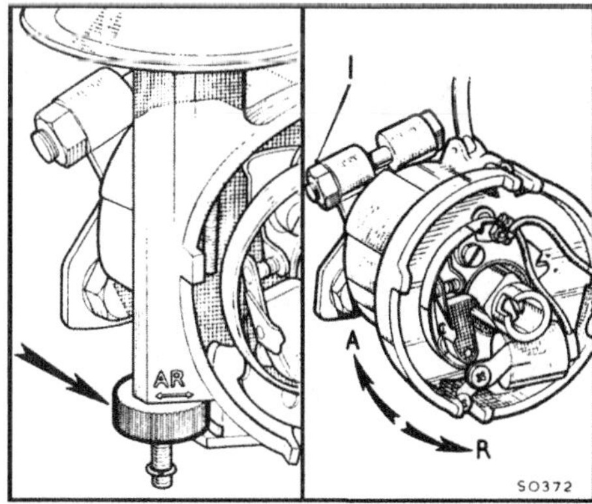

CARBURETTERS

Slow-running adjustment and synchronization Fig. 1

When the engine is fully run in the slow running may require adjustment. This must only be carried out when the engine has reached its normal running temperature.

As the needle size is determined during engine devlopment, tuning of the carburetters is confined to correct idling setting. Slacken the actuating arms on the throttle spindle interconnection. Close both throttles fully by unscrewing the throttle adjusting screws (1), then open each throttle by screwing down each screw one turn.

Remove the suction chamber (4) and piston assemblies, marking each to ensure replacement in their original positions, remove the air cleaner manifold and disconnect the mixture control cable. Screw the jet adjusting nuts (2) until each jet is flush with the bridge of its carburetter, or as near to this as possible (both jets being in the same relative position to the bridge of their respective carburetters). Refit the pistons and suction chamber assemblies, and check that the pistons fall freely onto the bridge of the carburetters (by means of the piston lifting pins (3)). Turn down each jet adjusting nut two complete turns (12 flats).

Restart the engine, and turn the throttle adjusting screws to give the desired idling speed by moving each screw an equal amount. By listening to the hiss in the intakes, adjust the throttle adjusting screws until the intensity of the hiss is similar on both intakes. This will synchronize the throttles.

When this is satisfactory, the mixture should be adjusted by screwing each jet adjusting nut (2), up to weaken, or down to enrich by the same amount until the fastest idling speed consistent with even firing is obtained. During this adjustment it is necessary to press the jets upwards and ensure that they are in contact with the adjusting nuts.

As the mixture is adjusted the engine will probably run faster and it may therefore be necessary to unscrew the throttle adjusting screws a little, each by the same amount, to reduce the speed.

Fig 1

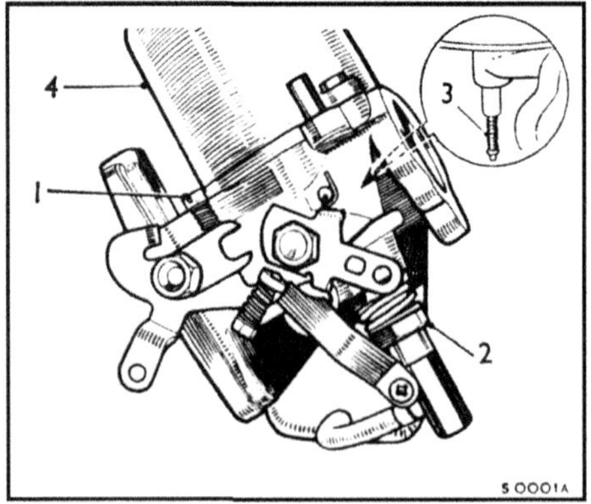

Fig. 2

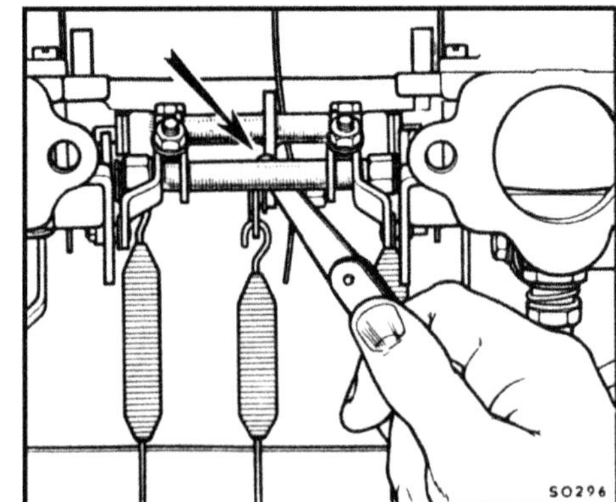

Now check the mixture strength by lifting the piston of the left-hand carburetter by approximately $\frac{1}{32}$ in. (·8 mm.) when:

(1) If the engine speed increases, the mixture strength of the front carburetter is too rich.

(2) If the engine speed immediately decreases, the mixture strength of the front carburetter is too weak.

(3) If the engine speed momentarily increases very slightly, the mixture strength of the front carburetter is correct.

Repeat the operation at the right-hand carburetter, and after adjustment re-check the left-hand carburetter, since both carburetters are interdependent.

When the mixture is correct the exhaust note should be regular and even. If it is irregular, with a splashy type of misfire and colourless exhaust, the mixture is too weak. If there is a regular or rhythmical type of misfire in the exhaust beat, together with a blackish exhaust, then the mixture is too rich.

Throttle linkage Fig. 2 Each throttle is operated by a lever and pin, with the pin working in a forked lever attached to the throttle spindle. A clearance exists between the pin and fork which must be maintained when the throttle is closed and the engine idling to prevent any load from the accelerator linkage being transferred to the throttle butterfly and spindle.

To set this clearance, with the throttle shaft levers free on the throttle shaft, put a ·012 in. (·3 mm.) feeler between the throttle shaft stop at the top and the choke control interconnecting rod. Move the throttle shaft lever downwards until the lever pin rests lightly on the lower arm of the fork in the carburetter throttle lever. Tighten the clamp bolt of the throttle shaft lever at this position. When both carburetters have been dealt with, remove the feeler. The pins on the throttle shaft should then have clearance in the forks.

Reconnect the mixture control cable, ensuring that the jet heads return against the lower face of the jet adjusting nuts when the mixture control is pushed fully in. Pull out the mixture control knob on the dash panel until the linkage is about to move the carburetter jets a minimum of $\frac{1}{4}$ in. (6 mm.) and adjust the fast-idle adjusting screws to give an engine speed of about 1,000 r.p.m. when hot.

Carburetters

Carburetters
Lubrication
Fig. 3
Each damper reservoir must be topped up periodically with thin engine oil. **Under no circumstances should heavy-bodied lubricant be used.** Unscrew the damper cap, withdraw the damper, and top up the reservoir until the oil level (arrowed) is $\frac{1}{2}$ in. (12 mm.) above the top of the hollow piston rod. Push the damper assembly back into position and screw the cap firmly into the reservoir.

Air cleaners
Fig. 4
The air cleaner covers and elements should only be removed when the elements are being renewed. To fit new elements, unscrew the wing nuts (1) from the top of the cleaner, withdraw the cover (2), and discard the elements (3). Thoroughly clean the container, fit new elements, and refit the cover and wing nuts.

Fig. 3

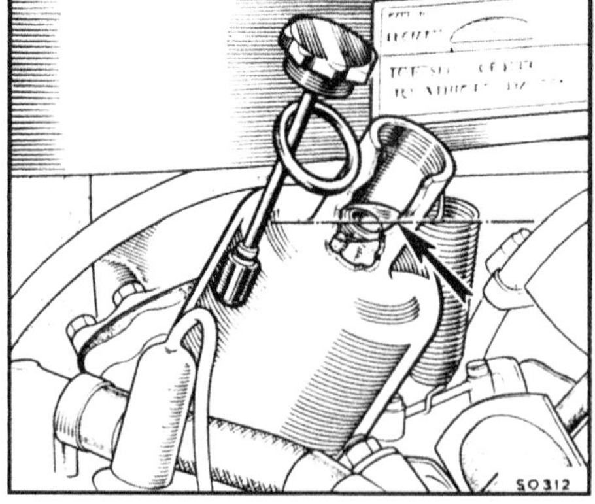

Fig. 4

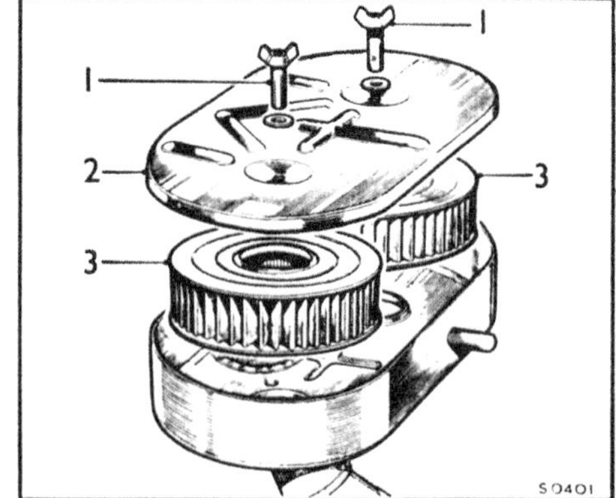

CLUTCH

Adjustment *Fig. 1*	It is important that a clearance should exist between the clutch thrust race and the thrust ring. All vehicles have this clearance carefully set before dispatch. Gradually, as wear takes place, however, this clearance will diminish and, if neglected, clutch slip will result.

An adjustable stop (1) is provided on the transmission casing just forward of the clutch operating lever (2). Pull the operating lever (2) outwards until all free movement is taken up and then check with a feeler gauge that there is a clearance of ·020 in. (·51 mm.) between the operating lever and the head of the adjustment bolt. Correct if necessary.

Clutch and brake master cylinders
Fig. 2

To check the level of the fluid in the brake (1) and clutch (2) master cylinder reservoirs, remove the plastic filler caps.

The fluid level must be maintained at the bottom of the filler neck; use only LOCKHEED DISC BRAKE FLUID (Series II) for topping up.

Fig. 1

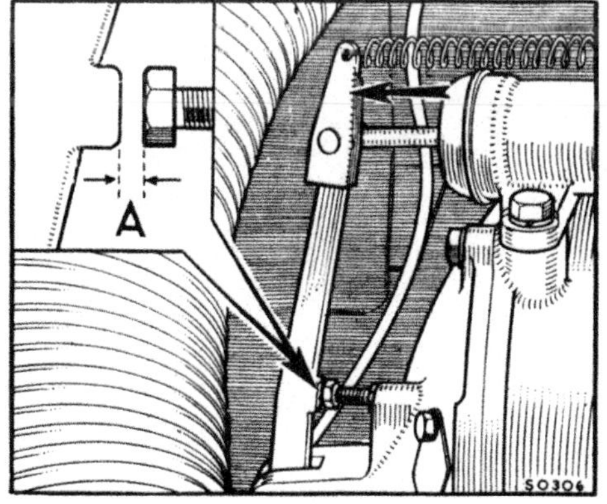

Fig. 2

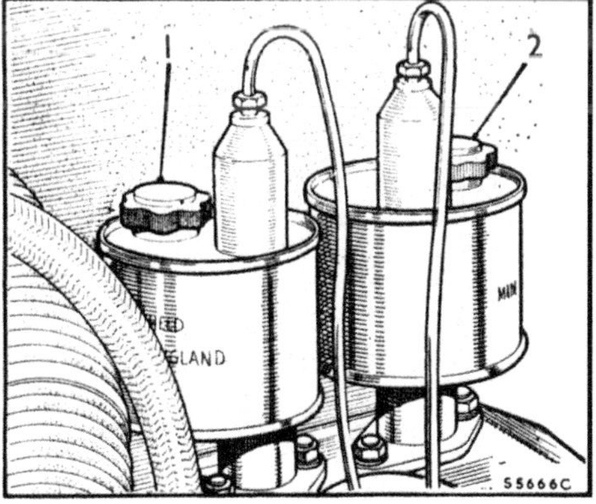

ENGINE/TRANSMISSION

Checking oil level
Fig. 1
The level of the oil in the engine sump is indicated by the dipstick (1) on the forward side of the engine. Maintain the level at the 'MAX' mark on the dipstick and never allow it to fall below the 'MIN' mark.

Fig. 4
The filler (1) is on the forward end of the rocker cover and is provided with a quick-action cap. The filler cap also incorporates a filter for the closed-circuit crankcase breathing intake.

Draining
Fig. 2
To drain the engine oil, remove the magnetic drain plug (arrowed) located on the right-hand side of the transmission casing. This operation should be carried out while the engine is warm.

Clean the drain plug; check that its copper sealing washer is in a satisfactory condition, and refit.

Filling
Fill with the correct quantity of oil (see 'GENERAL DATA'). Run the engine for a short while to recharge the filter then allow it to stand for a few minutes before checking the level with the dipstick.

The recommended oils are shown on page 56.

Oil filter
Fig. 3
The oil filter is of the renewable-element type. Release the filter bowl by unscrewing the retaining bolt.

Clean the bowl with fuel and dry it before fitting a new element.

The filter must be assembled in the order shown. Ensure that the seals are serviceable, and that the rubber seal (1) under the bolt head and the rubber or felt sealing ring (2) are a good fit on the bolt.

Remove the old and correctly position the new sealing ring (3) in the filter head and refit the filter assembly. Rotate the bowl while tightening to ensure that it is correctly located on the sealing ring (3) in the filter head. Check for oil leakage immediately the engine is started.

Fig. 1

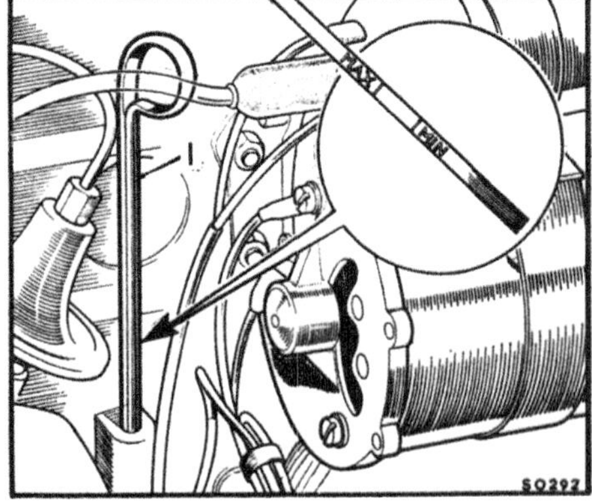

Fig. 2

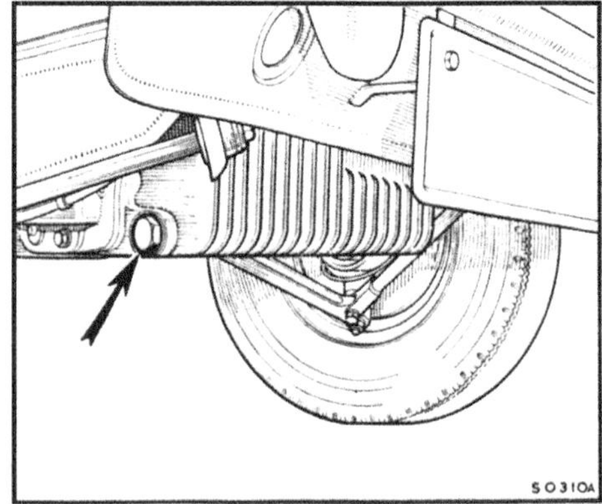

Engine breathing
Filler cap
Fig. 4

An air filter is incorporated in the oil filler cap (1), and is renewable as a complete assembly.

Control valve

Testing. With the engine at normal operating temperature, run it at idling speed. Remove the oil filler cap. If the valve is functioning correctly the engine speed will increase by approximately 200 r.p.m. as the cap is removed, the change in speed being audibly noticeable. If no change in speed occurs, service the valve as follows.

Servicing. Remove the spring clip (2) and dismantle the valve. Clean all metal parts with a solvent (trichlorethylene, fuel, etc.). If deposits are difficult to remove, immerse in boiling water before applying the solvent. Do not use an abrasive.

Clean the diaphragm (3) with detergent or methylated spirits.

Replace components showing signs of wear or damage.

Reassemble the valve, making sure the metering needle (4) is in the cruciform guides (5) and the diaphragm is seated correctly.

Fan belt
Checking

When correctly tensioned, a deflection, under moderate hand pressure, of $\frac{1}{2}$ in. (13 mm.) approximately should be possible at the midway point of the longest belt run between the pulleys.

Adjusting
Fig. 5

To adjust the belt tension, slacken the dynamo securing bolts (arrowed), and move the dynamo to the required position, using only hand pressure. Avoid overtensioning. Tighten the securing bolts.

Fig. 3

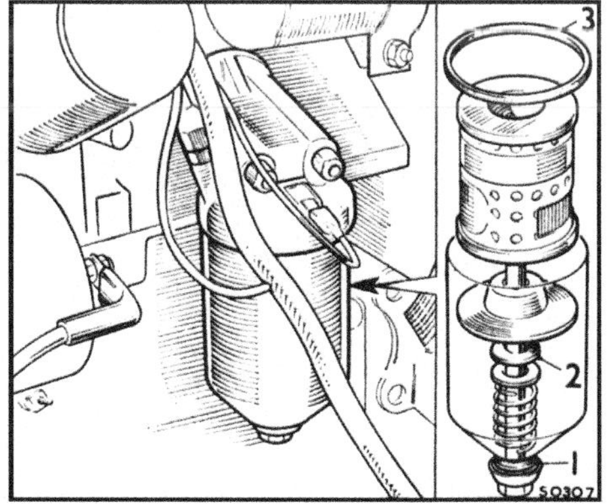

Fig. 4

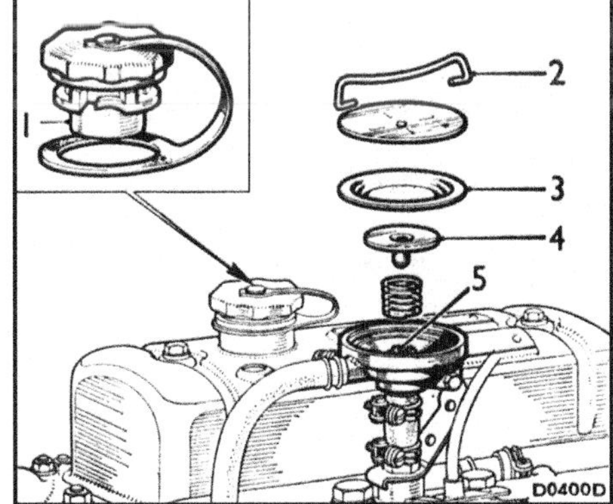

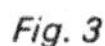

Valve rocker clearance
Checking
Fig. 6

Adjustment must be made with the tappet on the back of the cam, therefore the crankshaft must be rotated to bring each valve in turn to its checking position.

Unscrew the rocker cover retaining nuts, remove the rocker cover and insert a ·012 in. (·305 mm.) feeler gauge between the valve rocker arms and valve stems (inset). The gauge should be a sliding fit when the engine is cold. To rotate the crankshaft remove the sparking plugs, engage top gear and push the car forward.

Check each clearance in the following order:

Check No. 1 valve with No. 8 fully open. Check No. 8 valve with No. 1 fully open.

		3				6					6				3		
,,	,,	5	,,	,,	,,	4	,,	,,	,,	,,	4	,,	,,	,,	5	,,	,,
,,	,,	2	,,	,,	,,	7	,,	,,	,,	,,	7	,,	,,	,,	2	,,	,,

Adjusting

Slacken the adjusting screw locknut on the opposite end of the rocker arm and rotate the screw clockwise to reduce the clearance or anti-clockwise to increase it. Retighten the locknut when the clearance is correct, holding the screw against rotation with a screwdriver.

Check that its cork gasket is serviceable and refit the rocker cover.

Fig. 5

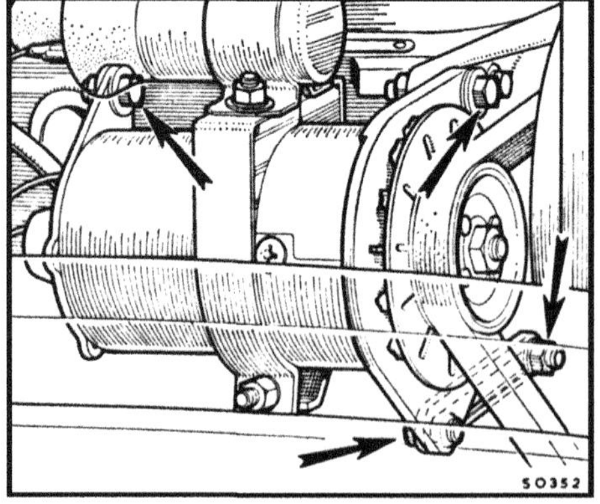

Fig. 6

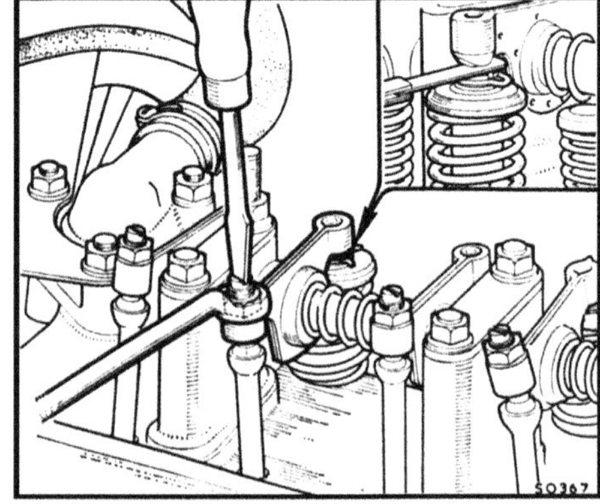

Suspension
Fig. 1

The suspension system employed on this vehicle is of the Hydrolastic type. After the first 12,000 miles (20000 km.) or 12 months the pressure in the system should be checked, and corrected if necessary.

All work connected with the system must be entrusted to a Distributor or Dealer. Under no circumstances must the system be tampered with, and the valves shown in the illustration must not be touched. The suspension system works under pressure, and it is important that the correct equipment is used when releasing the valve caps.

Should the Hydrolastic suspension system suffer damage and the fluid be lost, the suspension arms on the damaged side of the vehicle will contact the bump rubbers at both front and rear. In this condition the car may be driven with complete safety at 30 m.p.h. (50 km.p.h.) over matalled roads to the nearest Distributor or Dealer.

LUBRICATION

Swivel hub ball joints
Fig. 2

Two lubricating nipples (arrowed) are provided on each swivel hub. To lubricate, charge the nipples with one of the recommended greases. To ensure full penetration of the lubricant, this operation is best carried out with the car jacked up. If the nipples are already filled with grease no further grease can usually be forced in.

Front suspension
Fig. 3

Upper support arm inner pivot. A lubricating nipple is provided on each of the upper support arms. To lubricate, charge nipples with one of the recommended greases.

Fig. 1

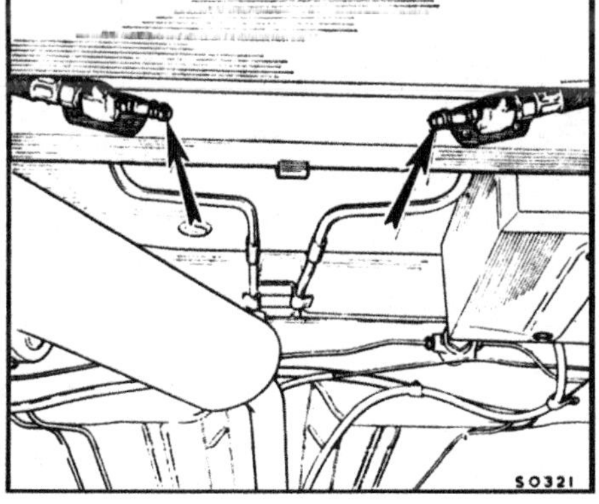

Fig. 2

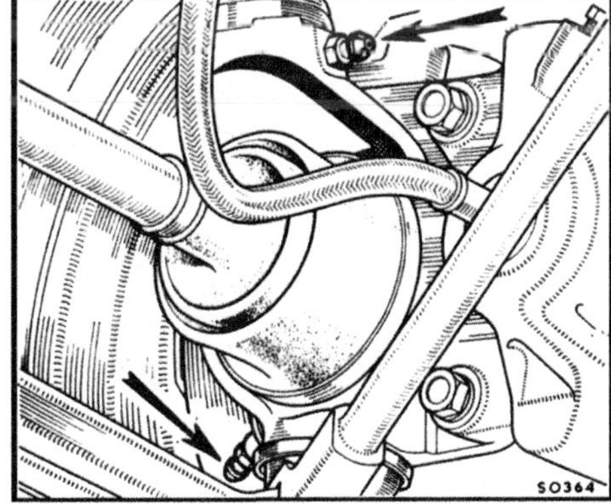

STEERING/SUSPENSION

Rear suspension radius arms
Fig. 4

A lubricating nipple is provided on each of the rear radius arms. To lubricate, charge the nipples with one of the recommended greases until excess grease appears from the inner bush.

Front wheel alignment

Incorrect front wheel alignment can cause excessive and uneven tyre wear.

Checking and resetting must be undertaken by your Distributor or Dealer, who will have all the information and equipment necessary for this work.
Incorrect adjustment could result in excessive articulation of the drive shaft joints, with consequent fouling of the suspension tie-rods by the road wheels when on full lock.

Fig. 3

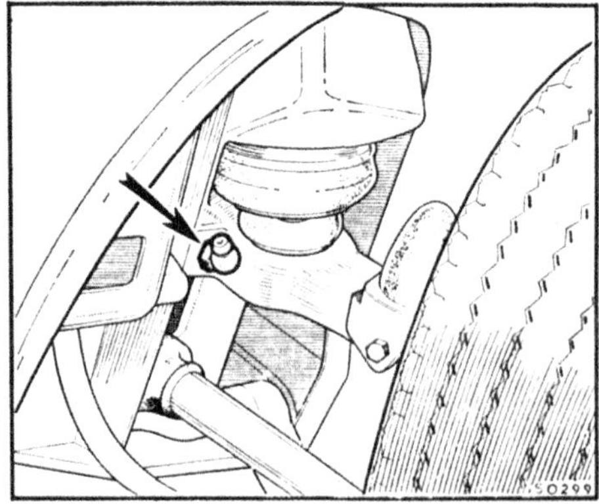

Fig. 4

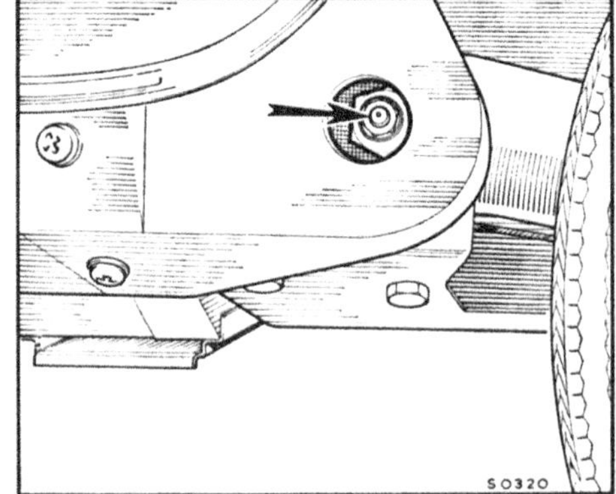

NOTES

GENERAL DATA

	COOPER		
Engine	Engine type	..	9FA
	Bore	..	2·543 in. (64·588 mm.)
	Stroke	..	3·00 in. (76·2 mm.)
	Cubic capacity	..	60·96 cu. in. (998 c.c.)
	Compression ratio	..	High 9 : 1. Low 7·8 : 1
	Firing order	..	1, 3, 4, 2
	Valve rocker clearance (cold)	..	·012 in. (·3 mm.)
	Idling setting	..	500 r.p.m. (hot)
	Oil pressure:		
	Normal (approx.)	..	40 to 60 lb./sq. in. (2·81 to 4·22 kg./cm.^{2})
	Idling (approx.)	..	15 lb./sq. in. (1·05 kg./cm.^{2})
Ignition	Sparking plugs	..	Champion N5, 14 mm.
	Sparking plug gap	..	·025 in. (·64 mm.)
	Static ignition timing:		
	High compression	..	5° B.T.D.C.
	Low compression	..	5° B.T.D.C.
	Stroboscopic ignition timing	..	7 to 7½° B.T.D.C. at 600 r.p.m.
	Contact breaker gap	..	014 to ·016 in. (·36 to ·40 mm.)
Fuel system	Carburetters	..	Twin S.U. type HS2
	Carburetter needles	..	Standard GY, Weak GG, Rich M
	Spring	..	Light blue
	Pump	..	S.U. (electric) type AUF 201
Transmission	Final drive ratio	..	3·765 : 1
	Overall gear ratios: First	..	12·05 : 1
	Second	..	7·214 : 1
	With Third	..	5·109 : 1
	synchromesh Fourth	..	3·765 : 1
	Reverse	..	12·05 : 1
Wheels and tyres	Wheel size	..	3·50B×10
	Tyre size and type	..	Dunlop SP41—Tubeless
	Tyre pressures (set cold):		
	All conditions: Front	..	28 lb./sq. in. (1·97 kg./cm.^{2})
	Rear	..	26 lb./sq. in. (1·83 kg./cm.^{2})

Dimensions	Track: Front	..	..	..	$47\frac{7}{16}$ in. (1·205 m.)
	Rear	..	..	..	$45\frac{5}{8}$ in. (1·164 m.)
	Turning circle	..	..	..	28 ft. 6 in. (8·55 m.)
	Front wheel alignment	..	..	$\frac{1}{16}$ in. (1·6 mm.) toe-out
	Wheelbase	..	..	..	6 ft. $8\frac{5}{32}$ in. (2·036 m.)
	Overall length	..	..	..	10 ft. $0\frac{1}{4}$ in. (3·05 m.)
	Overall width	..	..	..	4 ft. $7\frac{1}{2}$ in. (1·41 m.)
	Overall height	..	..	..	4 ft. 5 in. (1·35 m.)
	Ground clearance	..	..	..	$6\frac{5}{32}$ in. (15·63 cm.).

Capacities	Fuel tank	..	..	..	$5\frac{1}{2}$ gal. (25 litres, 6·6 U.S. gal.)
	Engine oil capacity (includes filter)				$8\frac{1}{2}$ pints (4·83 litres, 10·2 U.S. pints)
	Cooling system:				
	Without heater	..	..	..	$5\frac{1}{4}$ pints (3 litres, 6·3 U.S. pints)
	With heater	..	..	..	$6\frac{1}{4}$ pints (3·55 litres, 7·5 U.S. pints)

Weights	Maximum towing weight	..	..	8 cwt. (406·5 kg.)
	Weight (kerbside)	..	..	..	1,433 lb. (650 kg.)

General Data

Engine   **COOPER 'S'**

Engine type	.. .. ..	12FA (4-cylinder overhead valve)
Bore	.. ..	2·78 in. (70·61 mm.)
Stroke	.. ..	3·2 in. (81·28 mm.)
Cubic capacity	.. .. ..	77·9 cu. in. (1275 c.c.)
Compression ratio	.. ..	9·75 : 1
Firing order	.. .. ..	1, 3, 4, 2

Valve rocker clearance (cold) :

Competition	.. .. ..	·015 in. (·38 mm.)
Standard..	.. .. ..	·012 in. (·30 mm.)
Idling setting	.. .. ..	500 r.p.m. (hot)

Oil pressure :

Normal (approx.)	.. ..	40 to 70 lb./sq. in. (2·81 to 4·92 kg./cm.²)
Idling (approx.) ..	.. ..	15 lb./sq. in. (1·05 kg./cm.²)

Ignition

Sparking plugs	.. .. ..	Champion N 9Y, 14 mm.
Sparking plug gap ..	.. ..	·025 in. (·64 mm.)
Static ignition timing	..	2° B.T.D.C.
Stroboscopic ignition timing	..	4° B.T.D.C. at 600 r.p.m.
Contact breaker gap	..	·014 to ·016 in. (·36 to ·40 mm.)

Fuel system

Carburetters	.. .. ..	Twin S.U. type HS2
Carburetter needles	.. ..	Standard M, Weak EB, Rich AH2
Spring	.. ..	Red
Pump	.. ..	S.U. (Electric) type AUF 201

Wheels and tyres

Wheel sizes	.. .. ..	3·5B×10 or 4·5J×10
Tyre size and type : Standard	..	Dunlop 145—10SP, tubed
Optional	..	Dunlop 500L—10, tubed

Tyre pressures (set cold) :

Normal conditions : Front	..	28 lb./sq. in. (1·97 kg./cm.²)
Rear	..	26 lb./sq. in. (1·83 kg./cm.²)

Transmission   Overall gear ratios (as applicable)

Standard gearbox

Final drive ratio			*1st and reverse*	*2nd*	*3rd*	*4th*
3·765	.. ..	..	12·05 : 1	7·21 :·1	5·11 : 1	3·765 : 1
3·444	.. ..	..	11·02 : 1	6·60 : 1	4·67 : 1	3·444 : 1
3·938	.. ..	..	12·60 : 1	7·54 : 1	5·34 : 1	3·938 : 1
4·133	.. ..	..	13·27 : 1	7·92 : 1	5·61 : 1	4·133 : 1

Optional gearbox ratios:

Final drive ratio				*1st and reverse*	*2nd*	*3rd*	*4th*
3·765	..	..	..	9·66 : 1	6·70 : 1	4·68 : 1	3·765 : 1
3·444	..	..	..	8·84 : 1	6·13 : 1	4·27 : 1	3·444 : 1
3·938	..	..	..	10·12 : 1	7·02 : 1	6·89 : 1	3·938 : 1
4·133	..	..	..	10·61 : 1	7·35 : 1	5·13 : 1	4·133 : 1

Road speed in top at 1,000 r.p.m.

Final drive ratio					
3·765	..	..	..	..	14·7 m.p.h. (23·52 km.p.h.)
3·444	..	..	..	..	16·07 m.p.h. (25·71 km.p.h.)
3·939	..	..	..	..	14·06 m.p.h. (22·5 km.p.h.)
4·133	..	..	..	..	13·4 m.p.h. (21·44 km.p.h.)

Dimensions   Track: Front (3·5 in. rim) ..   .. $47\frac{17}{32}$ in. (1·207 m.)
  (4·5 in. rim) ..   .. $48\frac{17}{32}$ in. (1·233 m.)
Rear   (3·5 in. rim) ..   .. $46\frac{5}{16}$ in. (1·176 m.)
  (4·5 in. rim) ..   .. $47\frac{5}{16}$ in. (1·202 m.)
Turning circle   ..   ..   28 ft. 6 in. (8·55 m.)
Front wheel alignment   ..   .. $\frac{1}{16}$ in. (1·6 mm.) toe-out
Wheelbase   ..   ..   6 ft. $8\frac{5}{32}$ in. (2·036 m.)
Overall length   ..   ..   10 ft. $0\frac{1}{4}$ in. (3·05 m.)
Overall width   ..   ..   4 ft. $7\frac{1}{2}$ in. (1·41 m.)
Overall height   ..   ..   4 ft. 5 in. (1·35 m.)
Ground clearance (min.)   ..   .. $6\frac{5}{32}$ in. (15·63 cm.)

Capacities   Fuel (twin tanks)—total   ..   ..   11 gallons (13 U.S. gallons, 50 litres)
Engine oil capacity (includes filter) $8\frac{1}{2}$ pints (4·83 litres, 10·2 U.S. pints)
Cooling system:
Without heater   ..   ..   .. $5\frac{1}{4}$ pints (3 litres, 6·3 U.S. pints)
With heater   ..   ..   .. $6\frac{1}{4}$ pints (3·55 litres, 7·5 U.S. pints)

Weights   Maximum towing weight ..   ..   8 cwt. (406·5 kg.)
Weight (kerbside) ..   ..   ..   1,540 lb. (698 kg.) approx.

Detailed maintenance instructions will be found on the page given in brackets after each item.

Every week or before a long journey
Check oil level in engine/transmission unit. Top up if necessary. (40)
Test tyre pressures, and regulate if necessary. (22)
Check battery, and top up to correct level if necessary. (26)

	Every 3,000 miles (5000 km.) or 3 months	Every 6,000 miles (10000 km.) or 6 months	Every 12,000 miles (20000 km.) or 12 months
Engine			
Top up carburetter piston dampers. (38)	X	X	X
Check valve rocker clearances, and adjust if necessary.*		X	X
Fit new oil filler cap and filter assembly. (41)			X
Test and clean breather control valve. (41)			X
Check fan belt tension. (41)		X	X
Fit new air cleaner elements. (38)			X
Check coolant level in radiator, and top up if necessary. (19)	X	X	X
Top up windscreen washer bottle	X	X	X
Ignition			
Check functioning of automatic advance and retard mechanism. (33)		X	X
Lubricate all distributor parts as necessary. (34)		X	X
Check distributor contact points, clean, and adjust if necessary. (35)		X	X
Clean and adjust sparking plugs. (34)		X	
Fit new sparking plugs. (34)			X
Clutch			
Check level of fluid in hydraulic clutch supply tank, and top up. (39)	X	X	X
Check clearance at return stop, and adjust if necessary. (39)		X	X
Steering			
Check steering and suspension moving parts for wear.*			X
Check wheel alignment, and adjust if necessary.*		X	X
Check tightness of steering column clamp bolt.*	X	X	X

Brakes			
Inspect and blow out rear linings and drums. (25)			X
Check brake pedal travel, and adjust rear brakes if necessary. (24)	X	X	X
Check level of fluid in hydraulic brake supply tank. (39)	X	X	X
Make visual inspection of brake pipes and hoses.*	X	X	X
Inspect front disc brake pads for unequal wear. (24)		X	X
General			
Check tightness of nuts and bolts on suspension and universal joints.*		X	X
Electrical			
Check battery cell specific gravity readings and top up to correct level. (26)*	X	X	X
Check all lamps for correct functioning. (28)		X	X
Check headlamp alignment. (29)	X	X	X
Lubrication			
Check oil level in engine/transmission unit, and top up if necessary. (40)	X	X	X
Change engine/transmission oil if using monograde oil. (40)	X	X	X
Drain oil from engine/transmission unit, and refill with fresh oil. (40)		X	X
Fit new oil filter element. (40)		X	X
Lubricate door locks and hinges. (14)		X	X
Wheels and tyres			
Check tyre pressures, including spare. (22)	X	X	X

* Your Distributor or Dealer should check these items

NOTE.—Take the advice of your Distributor or Dealer on the need for:

1. More frequent engine oil changes;
2. Changing round road wheels.

BMC SERVICE

Identification
When communicating with your Distributor or Dealer always quote the commission, car, and engine numbers. When the communication concerns the transmission units or body details it is also necessary to quote the transmission casing and body numbers.

Commission number. Stamped on a plate fixed to the right-hand wing valance.

Car number. Located on a plate mounted between the radiator and the left-hand wing valance.

Engine number. Stamped on a metal plate fixed to the right-hand side of the cylinder block.
Transmission casing assembly. Stamped on a facing provided on the casing just below the starter motor.

Body number. Stamped on a metal plate fixed to grille panel stiffener.

Warranty
By keeping the Passport to Service, signed by the Distributor, Dealer, or vendor, in the vehicle you can quickly establish the date of purchase and provide the necessary details if adjustments are required to be carried out under warranty.

Claims for the replacement of parts under warranty must be submitted to the supplying Distributor or Dealer or, when this is not possible, to the nearest Distributor or Dealer, informing them of the vendor's name and address. Except in cases of emergency warranty work should always be carried out by a BMC appointed Distributor or Dealer.

Service Parts
When Service Parts are required insist on BMC GENUINE PARTS as these are designed and tested for your vehicle and in addition have the full backing of the BMC Factory Warranty. ONLY WHEN GENUINE PARTS ARE USED CAN BMC ACCEPT RESPONSIBILITY.

All BMC GENUINE PARTS and APPROVED ACCESSORIES can be identified by this label on the packing.

LUBRICATION

Weekly

(1)   ENGINE. Inspect the oil level by the dipstick, and replenish if necessary with oil to Ref. A.

Every 3,000 miles (5000 km.) or 3 months

(2)   ENGINE (if using monograde or single-viscosity oils only). Drain, and refill with fresh oil.

(3)   STEERING JOINTS.

(4)   REAR SUSPENSION. RADIUS ARMS.

} Give three or four strokes of the grease gun filled to Ref. B.

(5)   CARBURETTERS. Top up damper assembly reservoirs with oil to Ref. A.

Every 6,000 miles (10000 km.) or 6 months

(6)   ENGINE. Drain off the old oil and refill with fresh oil to Ref. A.

(7)   ENGINE. Fit a new oil filter element. (See page 40.)

(8)   DISTRIBUTOR. Lubricate all parts as necessary.

(9)   DYNAMO. Add a few drops of oil to Ref. A through the oil hole in the commutator end bearing.

AS INDICATED BY WARNING LIGHT

ENGINE. Fit a new oil filter element and change engine/transmission oil. (See page 40.)

NOTES:

The gear change shaft lubricating nipple shown on indicator 10 requires attention at major overhaul periods only, when grease to Ref. B should be used.

Oil and grease references are detailed on page **56.**

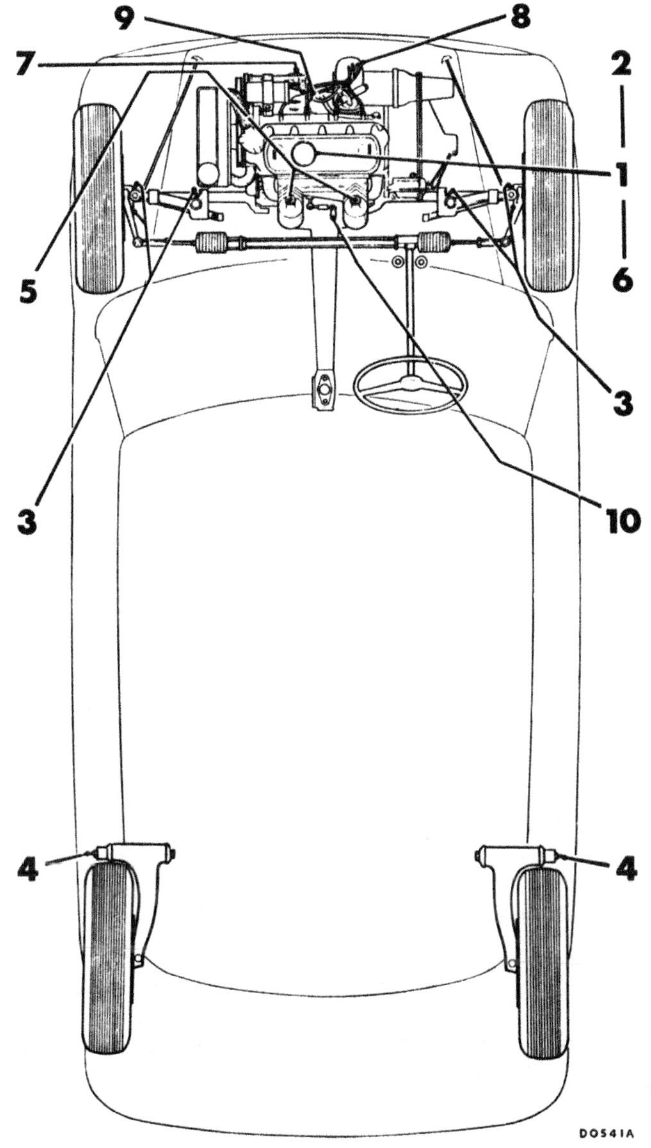

9
8
7
2
1
5
6
3
3
10
4
4
DOS41A

KEY TO RECOMMENDED LUBRICANTS

	A	B	C
Component	Engine/Transmission Unit, Oilcan, and Carburetters	Grease Points	Upper Cylinder Lubrication
Climatic conditions	All temperatures above −18° C, (0° F.)	All conditions	All conditions
FILTRATE	Filtrate 10W/30 Multigrade	Filtrate Super Lithium Grease	Filtrate Petroyle
STERNOL	Sternol W.W. Multigrade 10W/40	Ambroline L.H.T.	Sternol Magikoyl
DUCKHAM'S	Q. 5500	Duckham's L.B. 10 Grease	Duckham's Adcoid Liquid
CASTROL	Castrolite	Castrolease L.M.	Castrollo
ESSO	Esso Extra Motor Oil 10W/30	Esso Multipurpose Grease H	Esso Upper Cylinder Lubricant
MOBIL	Mobiloil Special 10W/30 or Mobiloil Super 10W/40	Mobilgrease M.P.	Mobil Upperlube
BP	Super Visco-Static 10W/40 or Visco-Static	Energrease L. 2	BP Upper Cylinder Lubricant
SHELL	Shell Super Motor Oil	Shell Retinax A	Shell Upper Cylinder Lubricant

Approval is also given to BP Super Visco-Static 20W/50, Shell X-100 Multigrade 20W/50, Sternol WW Multigrade 20W/50, Esso Extra Motor Oil 20W/40, Filtrate 20W/50, Mobiloil Special 20W/40, Castrol XL, and Duckham's Q.20–50. for temperatures down to −12° C. (10° F.) and to monograde or single-viscosity detergent/dispersant lubricants supplied by companies listed above.

For temperatures below −18° C. or 0° F., use multigrade S.A.E. 5W/20 or 5W/30 oil.

Brooklands Books Ltd., PO Box 904,
Amersham, HP6 9JA, England
brooklandsbooks.com

ISBN 9781855200210   Ref: M15HH   Part Number: AKD 4997   9W5/2429

Printed in Dunstable, United Kingdom